Celebrate with *Country Woman Christmas 2001!*

Rural homesteads twinkling in lights…wide-eyed children hanging ornaments on a tree…the sweet scent of cookies wafting from the oven. These oh-so-familiar images and aromas can only signal one thing—Christmas is just around the corner!

Nothing quite compares to this holiday, brimming with hope and happiness. To help you make the most of it, we've tied up a package of recipes, gift ideas and other goodies in our sixth edition of *Country Woman Christmas*.

What makes this annual book so special is its heartwarming country flavor. That's because most of the craft and food ideas, photos and stories come directly from the readers of *Country Woman* magazine.

Here's a peek at what you'll find waiting for you inside…

Taste Tempters. Everything to feed a hearty holiday appetite is here—appetizers, entrees, sweets and more. With over 100 recipes to choose from, you're sure to find an abundance of favorites that will live on Christmas after Christmas.

And because time is precious to busy country women, each dish has been taste- and time-tested in the *Country Woman* kitchen. The recipes within can also be made with ingredients you most likely have on hand, saving you a trip into town.

Holiday Handcrafts. The season isn't complete without at least one Christmas craft project. And you'll find a whole host of original ideas to choose from right here.

All are offered with easy-to-follow instructions, charts and patterns. Better yet, most can be completed in a few hours. Then just wrap up for gift giving or add them to your own homespun holiday decorations.

Plus you can read about country ladies who spread the spirit of the season throughout their homes—and learn how you can, too. Or you can share the nostalgic tales and other merry features with the rest of the family.

More in Store. With a colorful new edition added to this series each year, you can look forward to many more country-inspired festivities. But, for now, settle back and relish all the exciting ideas in *Country Woman Christmas 2001*. We hope you enjoy it as much as we enjoy bringing it to you!

Executive Editor
Kathy Pohl

Editor
Kathleen Anderson

Food Editor
Janaan Cunningham

Associate Food Editor
Coleen Martin

Senior Recipe Editor
Sue A. Jurack

Recipe Editor
Janet Briggs

Test Kitchen Assistant
Suzanne Hampton

Craft Editors
Jane Craig
Tricia Coogan

Associate Editors
Barbara Schuetz
Sharon Selz
Michelle Bretl
Jean Steiner
Susan Uphill

Editorial Assistant
Dorothy Paaske

Art Directors
Maribeth Greinke
Emma Acevedo

Art Associates
Tom Hunt
Sherri Harmon
Cathy Zoulek
Dena Ahlers
Jill Banks

Photographer
Rob Hagen
Dan Roberts

Food Photography Artist
Stephanie Marchese

Photo Studio Manager
Anne Schimmel

Production Assistants
Ellen Lloyd
Catherine Fletcher

© 2001 Reiman Publications, LLC
5400 S. 60th Street
Greendale WI 53129

International Standard
Book Number:
0-89821-315-0
International Standard
Serial Number:
1093-6750

INSIDE...

AND MUCH MORE!

PICTURED ON OUR COVER. Clockwise from top right: Simple Wooden Santa (p. 64), Pretty Patchwork Table Runner (p. 71) and Candy Cane Chalet (p. 48).

Joyous Season

Christmas with the snowflakes falling,
Candle glow and stars above;
Choirs singing 'neath the lamppost
Telling us that God is Love.

Christmas with the jeweled trees sparkling,
Manger scenes set in their place;
Mistletoe and wreaths of holly
Add a touch of festive grace.

Christmas with bright faces smiling,
Joy and gladness everywhere;
Spirit of goodwill and sharing
Now abides in hearts that care.

Christmas with the church bells ringing,
Candle glow and stars above—
Blessed symbols to remind us
Of God's wondrous gift of love.

—*Beverly J. Anderson, Ft. Lauderdale, Florida*

Carol's Heirloom Cookies Make Sweet Yule Scenes

COME holiday time, Carol Dillon's baking is molded in one task—creating eye-catching cookies that make a lasting and lip-smacking impression.

"My husband, Don, and I found a unique Christmas niche—making Springerle cookies," Carol confirms from the enterprising pair's Camp Hill, Pennsylvania acreage. "Don hand-carves molds out of basswood, and I stamp out picture-perfect confections.

"Legend has it that early Germans celebrated *Julfest* by making tiny cakes using wooden molds imprinted with animals, people, fruit, flowers, hearts and birds.

"Later, Springerle cookies commonly decorated Christmas trees, and the molds were displayed as artwork when not being used to make goodies."

The Dillons' modern Springerle business has shaped up to be a very sweet success…quite by accident, Carol admits.

"I purchased a small mold in Germany as a souvenir 30 years ago, not knowing its function. When I learned it was used to make Springerle cookies, I convinced Don to carve me more. We began taking orders, and now we're rolling out both molds and cookies for fun and profit."

Once Don finishes carving them, the molds go to the kitchen, Carol's favorite "stamping" ground. "After preparing the dough, I stamp it firmly with a floured mold to make a sharp imprint. Then I cut along the edges with a serrated roller," she notes.

"The formed cookie dough rises up as it bakes, which explains the name 'Springerle', German for 'little jumping horse'. While we sell our cookies plain, they can be painted with food coloring and threaded with ribbon for hanging."

To finish her baking blitz, Carol packages the merry masterpieces in tins to ship to old-fashioned snackers across the country. Batches of cookies have even been saved to decorate the Pennsylvania state Christmas tree at a display in Washington, D.C.

"These pale, hard cookies have a

RISING to the occasion, Carol Dillon (right) bakes up batches and batches of traditional German Springerle cookies using wooden molds carved by her husband, Don (below). And the sweet treats taste as good as they look!

pleasant lemon-anise flavor and are best dunked in cocoa, coffee or tea," Carol shares. "Many customers remember their grandmother making Springerle. Often, she'd have a special mold for each youngster."

In her household, the Springerle confections have been lifting spirits *and* cookie jar lids for generations, Carol confides. "Our two grown children and three grandsons all love the licorice-sweet taste, as does most everyone who tries them.

"If someone says they're too pretty to eat, I remind them that Springerle cookies are like all holiday memories," Carol warmly informs. "You can always make more!"

Editor's Note: *To receive a brochure with more information about Carol and Don's Springerle molds and cookies, send $1 (refundable with first order) and a self-addressed stamped envelope to D.D. Dillon Carvings, 850 Meadow Lane, Camp Hill PA 17011 or telephone 1-717/761-6895.*

WELCOME TO MY COUNTRY KITCHEN

By Christine Lockhart-Brown of Bladen, Nebraska

AS a girl, my grandmother trekked through her family's farm fields, collecting tumbleweeds to use in Christmas decorations. Nowadays, I'm sure she'd smile to see I've followed her lead in sprucing up my own home for the season!

Our family—husband Jim and I and sons Connor, 7, and Collin, 3—feel very fortunate to live in the house my grandparents built 80 years ago. That's obvious in how we trim our kitchen for the holidays, displaying my rural "roots" …quite naturally of course.

Wrapping the 15-foot by 14-foot room like a pretty package is a garland I accented with oven-dried apples and citrus and bunches of goldenrod I gleaned from our ditches. This earthy mix of materials makes a festive backsplash for our Formica countertops and spices up ceiling-tickling cupboards.

My father and granddad hand-built those cabinets—all 60 of them—out of white pine and plywood without using power tools! This time of year, I use the upper ones like a pantry to house my canning. Recently, Dad built me a matching island that's become the hub of our kitchen activities.

Traditionally, Jim and the boys hunt up the scraggliest little tree they can find for me to adorn with candy and plant atop the island. When I need that surface for serving, I set up cake pedestals that hold my homemade brownies, spiced cider, breads and cinnamon buns.

Elves Help with Holiday Baking

Many of these treats are the work of my special team of kitchen elves—our sons plus my young nieces and nephew. The fruits of their Yule labors include a frosted cookie tree, a gingerbread house and perky pretzel wreaths I rounded up above our kitchen window.

To carry on a homespun motif, I trimmed the window molding with reed baskets my grandmother made and a willow swag crafted by my sister. A delicate lace valance mimics the artwork Jack Frost paints on our north-facing panes.

Flanking a view of our fir windbreak are two built-in display shelves. They're the perfect place to showcase my collection of teapots. Beside the sink stands a cadre of watchful wooden Santas. Each represents a nationality in our family tree—Irish, Scottish, German, Swedish and Norwegian.

More memories of my heritage radiate from my great-grandmother's wood-burning cookstove. Although it works, I use it mainly for storage. In the warming cabinets I keep my cookbooks, and the oven holds tins of tea and coffee.

Adjacent is our handy desk/message center. I cheered it up with jolly hanging pots and a mini tree decked with cookie cutters. Our memo board is generally filled with our sons' wish lists, where Santa will be sure to see them.

Color Lends Festive Feeling

Actually, our kitchen is ready for Christmas year-round, thanks to its theme color—burgundy. It adds dash to our white cabinetry and flooring and coordinates with the forest green in my tablecloth and the wainscoting in our eating area.

The merry makings for the kitchen table's centerpiece are a lantern and a bowl of greens. (Jim says he's afraid to sit still, for fear I'll wrap him in greenery!) Overhead hangs an heirloom lamp, insuring sparkling dinner conversation.

Friends tell us our kitchen gives the message, "Come in and sit awhile." And that's exactly what we want it to say. A couple years ago, we welcomed a record number of guests—over 200 in one day. That was when we had the honor of being part of a holiday home tour for charity.

Of course, we cherish the visitors we get in any season. And even when the kitchen is filled to the brim with trimmings, there's always room for new friends like you!

YARDS OF GARLAND outline the spacious old-fashioned kitchen Christine Lockhart-Brown (shown at far left above) eagerly fills with holiday flavor each year. Wooden Santas, miniature evergreen trees, pretzel wreaths and a homemade gingerbread house blend with bits of memorabilia to season the room with holiday spirit.

MERRY MORNING TREATS. Clockwise from top left: Orange Blush (p. 11), Christmas Morning Frittata (p.11) and Sunny Pancakes (p.11).

Holiday Brunch

CHRISTMAS MORNING FRITTATA
Marlene Whyte, Tisdale, Saskatchewan
(Pictured on page 10)

Christmas breakfast is especially merry when this colorful frittata is on the menu. It's easy to assemble, so it's perfect for busy mornings.

    1 medium onion, chopped
    1 medium green pepper, chopped
    1 garlic clove, minced
    2 tablespoons butter *or* margarine
1/2 cup chopped tomatoes
1/4 cup minced fresh parsley
    5 eggs, lightly beaten
    2 cups (8 ounces) shredded mozzarella cheese
1/2 cup soft bread crumbs
    1 teaspoon Worcestershire sauce
1/2 to 1 teaspoon salt
1/4 teaspoon pepper

In a skillet, saute the onion, green pepper and garlic in butter for 5 minutes or until tender. Remove from the heat. Stir in tomatoes and parsley; set aside. In a large bowl, combine the remaining ingredients. Stir in reserved vegetables.

Pour into an ungreased 9-in. pie plate. Bake, uncovered, at 350° for 25-30 minutes or until a knife inserted near the center comes out clean. Let stand for 5 minutes before cutting. **Yield:** 6-8 servings.

SUNNY PANCAKES
Alecia Barlow, Fairborn, Ohio
(Pictured on page 10)

I found this recipe in an old cookbook given to me by my mother-in-law. The light, delicate pancakes have a nice citrus flavor that the tangy orange sauce complements.

1-1/4 cups all-purpose flour
    3 tablespoons sugar
2-1/2 teaspoons baking powder
  3/4 teaspoon salt
    1 egg
    1 cup orange juice
1/4 cup milk
    3 tablespoons vegetable oil
    2 to 3 teaspoons finely grated orange peel
ORANGE SAUCE:
1/2 cup sugar
    1 tablespoon cornstarch
1/4 teaspoon salt
3/4 cup water
1/2 cup orange juice
    2 tablespoons butter *or* margarine
    1 tablespoon lemon juice
    2 to 3 teaspoons finely grated orange peel

In a large bowl, combine the first four ingredients. In another bowl, combine the egg, orange juice, milk, oil and orange peel; add to dry ingredients just until moistened. Pour batter by 1/4 cupfuls onto a lightly greased hot griddle. Turn when bubbles form on top; cook until second side is golden brown.

For orange sauce, combine sugar, cornstarch and salt in a saucepan. Stir in the remaining ingredients. Bring to a boil; cook and stir for 2 minutes or until thickened. Serve warm with pancakes. **Yield:** 12 pancakes (about 1 cup sauce).

ORANGE BLUSH
Arsolia Hayden, Owenton, Kentucky
(Pictured on page 10)

Your taste buds will enjoy waking up to this drink. It's delicious and simple, yet it adds a special touch to any meal.

    1 can (12 ounces) frozen orange juice concentrate, thawed
    2 cups cranberry juice
1/2 cup sugar
    1 liter club soda, chilled
Crushed ice

In a large pitcher or bowl, combine the orange juice concentrate, cranberry juice and sugar. Refrigerate for at least 1 hour. Just before serving, stir in soda. Serve over ice. **Yield:** 6 cups.

PUMPKIN DOUGHNUT DROPS
Beva Staum, Muscoda, Wisconsin

I always have a few special treats handy when the grandchildren visit. These cake doughnuts are a favorite snack.

    2 eggs
1-1/4 cups sugar
    2 tablespoons shortening
    1 cup cooked *or* canned pumpkin
    2 teaspoons white vinegar
    1 teaspoon vanilla extract
    3 cups all-purpose flour
1/2 cup nonfat dry milk powder
    3 teaspoons baking powder
1/2 teaspoon salt
1/2 teaspoon ground cinnamon
1/2 teaspoon ground nutmeg
1/2 cup lemon-lime soda
Oil for deep-fat frying
Additional sugar

In a mixing bowl, beat the eggs, sugar and shortening. Add the pumpkin, vinegar and vanilla. Combine the dry ingredients; add to the pumpkin mixture alternately with soda. In an electric skillet or deep-fat fryer, heat oil to 375°. Drop teaspoonfuls of batter, a few at a time, into hot oil. Fry for 1 minute on each side or until golden brown. Drain on paper towels, roll in sugar while warm. **Yield:** about 7 dozen.

FRUITED AMBROSIA
Edie DeSpain, Logan, Utah

This is a great take-along dish for any Yuletide gathering. Crunchy nuts, chewy coconut and fruit galore provide a heavenly blend of textures and flavors.

    1 can (14 ounces) sweetened condensed milk
    1 cup (8 ounces) plain yogurt
  1/2 cup lime juice
    2 cans (11 ounces *each*) mandarin oranges, drained
    1 can (20 ounces) pineapple chunks, drained
1-1/2 cups halved green grapes
1-1/3 cups flaked coconut
    1 cup miniature marshmallows
    1 cup chopped pecans
  1/2 cup halved maraschino cherries, drained

In a large bowl, combine the milk, yogurt and lime juice. Stir in the remaining ingredients. Cover and refrigerate for up to 3 hours. **Yield:** 10-14 servings.

APRICOT CREAM-FILLED WAFFLES
Dorothy Smith, El Dorado, Arkansas

You'll have more time to open gifts when you make these simply scrumptious waffles for breakfast. The rich mixture is easy to whip up and can quickly be doubled for unexpected company.

    1 package (3 ounces) cream cheese, softened
    1 to 2 tablespoons honey
  2/3 cup chopped canned apricots
    8 frozen waffles, toasted
  1/2 cup maple syrup, warmed

In a small bowl, combine cream cheese and honey; mix well. Stir in apricots. Spread cream cheese mixture on four waffles; top with remaining waffles. Serve with syrup. **Yield:** 4 servings.

CRUMB-TOPPED BAKED PINEAPPLE
Alice Tatro, Geneva, Nebraska

Sweet fruit and a crunchy topping give this comforting side dish plenty of old-fashioned goodness. It's the perfect tummy warmer for any cold-weather occasion.

  1/2 cup sugar
    2 tablespoons all-purpose flour
    1 can (20 ounces) pineapple chunks, undrained
    1 cup (4 ounces) shredded cheddar cheese
  1/2 cup maraschino cherries, drained
  3/4 cup dry bread crumbs
    2 tablespoons butter *or* margarine, melted

In a large bowl, combine the sugar, flour and pineapple; mix well. Stir in cheese and cherries. Transfer to a greased 8-in. square baking dish. Toss bread crumbs and butter; sprinkle over top. Bake, uncovered, at 350° for 30-35 minutes or until golden brown and bubbly. Serve warm. **Yield:** 6-8 servings.

HAM AND BROCCOLI STRATA
Robin Friedly, Louisville, Kentucky

Entertaining is easy with this homespun strata that features broccoli, ham and cheese. You assemble it the night before you need it, so there's no last-minute fuss.

    2 packages (10 ounces *each*) frozen chopped
      broccoli, thawed and drained
  3/4 pound thinly sliced deli ham, cut into 1/2-inch
      strips
    2 cups (8 ounces) shredded Swiss cheese
    1 loaf (8 ounces) French bread, cut into 1-inch slices
    6 eggs, lightly beaten
    2 cups milk
    3 tablespoons dried minced onion
    3 tablespoons Dijon mustard
  1/2 teaspoon hot pepper sauce
  1/2 teaspoon paprika

Combine broccoli, ham and cheese; spread half into a greased 13-in. x 9-in. x 2-in. baking dish. Arrange bread slices on top. Cover with remaining broccoli mixture. In a bowl, combine the eggs, milk, onion, mustard and hot pepper sauce. Pour over broccoli mixture. Sprinkle with paprika. Cover and refrigerate overnight.

Remove from the refrigerator 30 minutes before baking. Bake, uncovered, at 350° for 35-40 minutes or until a knife inserted near the center comes out clean. Let stand for 5 minutes before serving. **Yield:** 12 servings.

OVERNIGHT STICKY ROLLS
K. Baldwin, Wildomar, California

Smiles will greet you when you serve these yummy rolls. Seasoned with cinnamon and baked in a rich, gooey syrup, the goodies please everyone I know!

5-1/2 to 6 cups all-purpose flour
    2 tablespoons sugar
    2 packages (1/4 ounce *each*) active dry yeast
    2 teaspoons salt
1-3/4 cups milk
  1/2 cup water
    3 tablespoons shortening
  3/4 cup butter *or* margarine, *divided*
    1 cup packed brown sugar
    2 tablespoons corn syrup
    1 cup pecan halves *or* walnut pieces
FILLING:
  1/2 cup sugar
    1 teaspoon ground cinnamon

In a mixing bowl, combine 2-1/2 cups flour, sugar, yeast and salt. In a saucepan, heat milk, water and shortening to 120°-130°. Add to the flour mixture. Beat on low speed for 2 minutes; beat on medium for 3 minutes. Add enough remaining flour to form a soft dough. Turn onto a floured surface; knead until smooth and elastic, about 6-8 minutes. Place in a greased bowl, turning once to grease top. Cover and let rise in a warm place until doubled, about 1 hour.

Meanwhile, in a saucepan, combine 1/2 cup butter, brown sugar and corn syrup. Cook and stir over medium-low heat until sugar is dissolved and butter is melted. Pour into two greased 13-in. x 9-in. x 2-in. baking pans. Sprinkle with pecans.

Punch dough down. Turn onto a floured surface; divide dough in half. Roll each portion into a 12-in. x 8-in. rectangle. Spread with remaining butter to within 1/2 in. of edges. Combine sugar and cinnamon; sprinkle over butter. Roll up, jelly-roll style, starting with a long side; pinch seams to seal.

Cut into 1-in. slices. Place rolls, cut side down, in prepared pans. Cover and refrigerate overnight. Remove from the refrigerator 20 minutes before baking. Bake at 400° for 20-25 minutes or until golden brown. Invert rolls onto a serving platter. **Yield:** 2 dozen.

CRUNCHY ORANGE MUFFINS
Audrey Thibodeau, Fountain Hills, Arizona

The topping on these muffins reminds me of a crumb cake. I like to bake a big batch and store some in the freezer to serve to guests.

      1 cup all-purpose flour
  1/2 cup whole wheat flour
  1/2 cup packed brown sugar
      2 teaspoons baking powder
      1 teaspoon ground cinnamon
  1/4 teaspoon salt
  1/4 teaspoon ground nutmeg
      1 egg
  1/2 cup vegetable oil
  1/2 cup orange juice
      1 tablespoon grated orange peel
STREUSEL TOPPING:
  1/2 cup packed brown sugar
  1/2 cup chopped pecans
  1/4 cup all-purpose flour
      2 tablespoons butter *or* margarine, melted
      1 teaspoon ground cinnamon

In a large bowl, combine the first seven ingredients. In a small bowl, combine the egg, oil, orange juice and peel; stir into dry ingredients just until moistened. Fill greased muffin cups two-thirds full.

Combine topping ingredients; sprinkle heaping tablespoonfuls on each muffin. Bake at 375° for 18-20 minutes or until a toothpick comes out clean. Cool for 5 minutes before removing from pan to a wire rack. **Yield:** 1 dozen.

CRANBERRY BANANA COFFEE CAKE
Gloria Friesen, Casper, Wyoming

I make this moist cake for Christmas morning every year. It tastes like banana bread but has a sweet golden topping with a nutty crunch.

  1/2 cup butter *or* margarine, softened
  1/2 cup sugar
      2 eggs
      1 teaspoon vanilla extract
      2 cups all-purpose flour
      2 teaspoons baking powder
      1 teaspoon ground cinnamon

  1/4 teaspoon salt
  1/4 teaspoon ground allspice
      2 medium ripe bananas, mashed (about 3/4 cup)
      1 cup whole-berry cranberry sauce
TOPPING:
  1/2 cup packed brown sugar
  1/2 cup chopped pecans
      2 tablespoons all-purpose flour
      2 tablespoons butter *or* margarine, melted

In a large mixing bowl, cream the butter and sugar. Beat in eggs and vanilla. Combine the dry ingredients; add to the creamed mixture alternately with bananas. Spread into a greased 13-in. x 9-in. x 2-in. baking pan. Top with cranberry sauce.

In a small bowl, combine brown sugar, pecans and flour; stir in butter. Sprinkle over cranberries. Bake at 350° for 45-50 minutes or until a toothpick inserted near the center comes out clean. Cool in pan on a wire rack. **Yield:** 12-15 servings.

BREAKFAST SAUSAGE RING
Elsie Hofe, Littlestown, Pennsylvania

My daughter found this hearty sausage and egg recipe years ago, and our family loves it. It's baked in a ring mold and adds a festive flair to any holiday table.

      2 eggs
1-1/2 cups soft bread crumbs, toasted
  1/4 cup chopped onion
  1/4 cup minced fresh parsley
      2 pounds bulk sage pork sausage
Scrambled eggs
Pimiento strips and additional parsley, optional

In a bowl, combine the eggs, bread crumbs, onion and parsley. Add sausage; mix well. Pat into a greased 6-cup ring mold. Bake at 350° for 20 minutes; drain. Bake 20-25 minutes longer or until juices run clear. Drain; unmold onto a serving platter. Fill with scrambled eggs. Garnish with pimientos and parsley if desired. **Yield:** 8 servings.

HOMEMADE PANCAKE SYRUP
Jill Hanns, Klamath Falls, Oregon

This simple maple syrup cooks up in minutes but leaves a lasting impression. It's best served hot over waffles or pancakes with lots of creamy butter.

  3/4 cup packed brown sugar
  1/4 cup sugar
  3/4 cup water
  1/2 cup light corn syrup
  1/2 teaspoon maple flavoring
  1/2 teaspoon vanilla extract

In a saucepan, combine the sugars, water and corn syrup; bring to a boil over medium heat. Boil for 7 minutes or until slightly thickened. Remove from the heat; stir in maple flavoring and vanilla. Cool for 15 minutes. Serve over pancakes, waffles or French toast. **Yield:** about 1-1/2 cups.

Christmas Breads

SPICY PUMPKIN BREAD
Paula Cronk, Lander, Wyoming
(Pictured on page 16)

I like anything made with pumpkin, but this tender loaf is irresistible. Sometimes, I'll top it with a spicy glaze that features nutmeg and cinnamon.

    1 cup butter *or* margarine, softened
    2 cups sugar
    4 eggs
    2 cups cooked *or* canned pumpkin
    2 teaspoons vanilla extract
3-3/4 cups all-purpose flour
    2 teaspoons baking soda
    2 teaspoons ground cinnamon
    1 teaspoon salt
    1 teaspoon ground nutmeg
1/2 teaspoon ground cloves
1/2 teaspoon ground ginger
    2 cups (12 ounces) semisweet chocolate chips
    1 cup chopped walnuts
GLAZE (optional):
    1 cup confectioners' sugar
    2 tablespoons hot water
1/4 teaspoon ground nutmeg
1/4 teaspoon ground cinnamon
Dash ground cloves

In a large mixing bowl, cream butter and sugar. Add eggs, one at a time, beating well after each addition. Add pumpkin and vanilla; mix well. Combine the dry ingredients. Stir into pumpkin mixture just until moistened. Fold in chocolate chips and walnuts.

Spoon into two greased 8-in. x 4-in. x 2-in. loaf pans. Bake at 350° for 65-75 minutes or until a toothpick inserted near the center comes out clean. Cool for 10 minutes before removing from pans to wire racks. If desired, combine glaze ingredients; drizzle over cooled loaves. **Yield:** 2 loaves.

CRANBERRY APRICOT SCONES
Karin Bailey, Golden, Colorado
(Pictured on page 16)

Dried apricots and cranberries and a bit of grated orange peel give these golden scones plenty of fruity flavor. They're perfect served with a mug of hot coffee or tea.

    3 cups all-purpose flour
1/3 cup sugar
    1 tablespoon baking powder
1/2 teaspoon baking soda
1/4 teaspoon salt
    6 tablespoons cold butter *or* margarine
1/3 cup chopped dried apricots
1/3 cup dried cranberries
3/4 cup buttermilk
    1 egg
    1 egg white

    2 teaspoons grated orange peel
Additional sugar

In a bowl, combine the dry ingredients. Cut in butter until mixture resembles fine crumbs. Stir in apricots and cranberries. In a bowl, combine the buttermilk, egg, egg white and orange peel; stir into crumb mixture just until blended.

Turn onto a floured surface; knead gently four times. Roll into a 12-in. x 6-in. rectangle. Cut into eight 3-in. squares. Cut each square into two triangles. Separate pieces and transfer to a greased baking sheet. Sprinkle with additional sugar. Bake at 400° for 12-15 minutes or until browned. Serve warm. **Yield:** 16 scones.

PULL-APART BACON BREAD
Cathy Steinkuhler, Burr, Nebraska

To dress up plain recipes, I'll toss a bit of bacon into the mix, just like I did here. I'm always pleased with the results! Pieces of this hearty bread are almost a meal in themselves.

3/4 cup finely chopped onion
3/4 cup finely chopped green pepper
    1 teaspoon vegetable oil
    3 tubes (7-1/2 ounces *each*) refrigerated
        buttermilk biscuits
    1 pound sliced bacon, cooked and crumbled
1/2 cup butter *or* margarine, melted
1/2 cup shredded cheddar cheese

In a small skillet, saute onion and green pepper in oil until tender. Cut each biscuit into quarters. In a large bowl, gently toss onion mixture, biscuits, bacon, butter and cheese until combined. Transfer to a greased 10-in. tube pan. Bake at 350° for 25-30 minutes or until golden brown. Immediately invert onto a serving plate. Serve warm. Refrigerate leftovers. **Yield:** 10-12 servings.

DANISH JULEKAGE
Phyllis Levendusky, Osage, Iowa
(Pictured on page 17)

Cardamom and lots of fruit enliven this unique holiday bread. The recipe was handed down from my grandmother, who came to the United States from Denmark when she was 16 years old.

    2 packages (1/4 ounce *each*) active dry yeast
1/4 cup warm water (110° to 115°)
    2 cups warm milk (110° to 115°)
    1 cup sugar
1/2 cup butter *or* margarine, softened
    1 tablespoon shortening
    2 teaspoons salt
    1 teaspoon ground cardamom
    3 eggs, beaten
8-1/2 to 9 cups all-purpose flour
    1 cup raisins

1 cup chopped candied fruit
FILLING:
    2 tablespoons butter *or* margarine, melted
1/4 cup sugar
TOPPING:
    1/4 cup sugar
    2 tablespoons all-purpose flour
1/2 teaspoon ground cardamom
    2 tablespoons cold butter *or* margarine

In a mixing bowl, dissolve yeast in warm water. Add milk, sugar, butter, shortening, salt, cardamom, eggs and 4 cups flour; beat until smooth. Stir in raisins, candied fruit and enough remaining flour to form a soft dough.

Turn onto a floured surface; knead until smooth and elastic, about 6-8 minutes. Place in a greased bowl, turning once to grease top. Cover and let rise in a warm place until doubled, about 1-1/4 hours.

Punch dough down. Turn onto a lightly floured surface; divide in half. Roll each portion into a 12-in. x 9-in. rectangle. Brush with butter; sprinkle with sugar to within 1/2 in. of edges. Roll up, jelly-roll style, starting with a long side; pinch seams to seal and tuck ends under. Place, seam side down, in two greased 9-in. x 5-in. x 3-in. loaf pans. Cover and let rise until doubled, about 45 minutes.

For topping, combine the sugar, flour and cardamom; cut in butter until mixture resembles coarse crumbs. Sprinkle over loaves. Bake at 350° for 50-60 minutes or until golden brown. Remove from pans to cool on wire racks. **Yield:** 2 loaves.

ANGEL YEAST BISCUITS
Karen Regennitter, Ritzville, Washington

These versatile biscuits are so light, they almost melt in your mouth. They can be served with a sweet topping like jelly or a savory scoop of sausage gravy.

    1 package (1/4 ounce) active dry yeast
1/4 cup warm water (110° to 115°)
    1 tablespoon sugar
3/4 cup warm buttermilk* (110° to 115°)
    3 cups all-purpose flour
    2 teaspoons baking powder
3/4 teaspoon salt
1/2 teaspoon baking soda
1/2 cup cold butter (no substitutes)

In a bowl, dissolve yeast in warm water. Add sugar; let stand for 5 minutes. Stir in buttermilk; set aside. In a bowl, combine the flour, baking powder, salt and baking soda. Cut in butter until mixture resembles coarse crumbs. Stir in yeast mixture; mix well. Turn onto a floured surface; gently knead for 1 minute. Place in a greased bowl, turning once to grease top. Cover and let rise in a warm place until doubled, about 30 minutes.

Punch dough down. Turn onto a lightly floured surface; roll to 3/4-in. thickness. Cut with a floured 2-1/2-in. round biscuit cutter. Place 2 in. apart on a greased baking sheet. Prick tops with a fork. Cover and let rise until doubled, about 45 minutes. Bake at 375° for 15-18 minutes or until golden brown. Remove from pan to cool on a wire rack. Serve warm. **Yield:** 1 dozen.

*Editor's Note: Warm buttermilk will appear curdled.

POINSETTIA COFFEE CAKE
Rowena Wilson, Jetmore, Kansas
(Pictured below)

I often take this yeasty coffee cake to Christmas open houses or church functions. People "ooh" and "aah" over the fun poinsettia shape, but that doesn't stop them from cutting big pieces.

    1 package (1/4 ounce) active dry yeast
1/4 cup warm water (110° to 115°)
3/4 cup warm milk (110° to 115°)
    3 eggs, beaten
1/3 cup sugar
    2 teaspoons grated lemon peel
    1 teaspoon salt
    5 to 5-1/2 cups all-purpose flour
3/4 cup chopped dates
1/2 cup chopped nuts
FROSTING:
    1 tablespoon butter *or* margarine, softened
    1 cup confectioners' sugar
3/4 teaspoon vanilla extract
    3 to 4 teaspoons water
Yellow and red colored sugar

In a mixing bowl, dissolve yeast in warm water. Add milk, eggs, sugar, lemon peel, salt and 2-1/2 cups flour; beat until smooth. Stir in dates and nuts. Stir in enough remaining flour to form a soft dough. Turn onto a floured surface; knead until smooth and elastic, about 6-8 minutes. Place in a greased bowl, turning once to grease top. Cover and let rise in a warm place until doubled, about 1-1/2 hours.

Punch dough down. Turn onto a floured surface; divide into eight equal pieces. Shape one piece into eight smaller balls; mound in the center of a large greased baking sheet. Form remaining pieces into teardrop shapes by tapering one side of each ball. Place around smaller balls with wide end of petals touching the flower center. Cover and let rise until doubled, about 30 minutes.

Bake at 350° for 20-25 minutes or until golden brown. Cool slightly. Meanwhile, in a mixing bowl, combine butter, confectioners' sugar, vanilla and enough water to achieve desired frosting consistency. Spread over warm coffee cake. Sprinkle center with yellow sugar and petals with red sugar. **Yield:** 16-18 servings.

Editor's Note: This coffee cake dough contains no butter, shortening or oil.

FESTIVE BREADS. Shown clockwise from top left: Cran-Apple Muffins (p. 18), Danish Julekage (p. 14), Braided Egg Bread (p.18), Cranberry Apricot Scones (p. 14) and Spicy Pumpkin Bread (p. 14).

CRAN-APPLE MUFFINS
Millie Westland, Hayward, Minnesota
(Pictured on page 16)

I like to pile these muffins on a plate when friends drop in for coffee. Even my grandkids enjoy the nice flavor combination.

    1/2 cup whole-berry cranberry sauce
    1/2 teaspoon grated orange peel
1-1/2 cups all-purpose flour
    1/2 cup sugar
      1 teaspoon ground cinnamon
    1/2 teaspoon baking soda
    1/4 teaspoon baking powder
    1/4 teaspoon salt
      1 egg
    1/3 cup milk
    1/3 cup vegetable oil
      1 cup shredded peeled tart apple
    1/2 cup confectioners' sugar
      1 tablespoon orange juice

In a small bowl, combine cranberry sauce and orange peel; set aside. In a large bowl, combine the flour, sugar, cinnamon, baking soda, baking powder and salt. Beat the egg, milk and oil; stir into dry ingredients just until moistened. Fold in apple. Fill greased or paper-lined muffin cups half full.

Make a well in the center of each muffin; fill with about 2 teaspoons of reserved cranberry mixture. Bake at 375° for 18-20 minutes or until a toothpick inserted in muffin comes out clean. Cool for 5 minutes before removing from pan to a wire rack. Combine confectioners' sugar and orange juice; drizzle over cooled muffins. **Yield:** about 1 dozen.

BRAIDED EGG BREAD
Marlene Jeffrey, Holland, Manitoba
(Pictured on page 17)

Since I first made this bread a few years ago, it's become a much-requested recipe. I'm sure I'll pass it down to future generations.

3-1/4 to 3-3/4 cups all-purpose flour
      1 tablespoon sugar
      1 package (1/4 ounce) active dry yeast
    3/4 teaspoon salt
    3/4 cup water
      3 tablespoons vegetable oil
      2 eggs
TOPPING:
      1 egg
      1 teaspoon water
    1/2 teaspoon poppy seeds

In a mixing bowl, combine 1-1/2 cups flour, sugar, yeast and salt. In a saucepan, heat water and oil to 120°-130°. Add to dry ingredients with eggs and blend well. Beat on medium speed for 3 minutes. Stir in enough remaining flour to form a soft dough. Turn onto a floured surface; knead until smooth and elastic, about 6-8 minutes. Place in a greased bowl, turning once to grease top. Cover and let rise in a warm place until doubled, about 1-1/2 hours.

Punch dough down. Set a third of the dough aside. Divide remaining dough into three pieces. Shape each portion into a 13-in. rope. Place ropes on a greased baking sheet and braid; pinch ends to seal and tuck under. Divide reserved dough into three equal pieces; shape each into a 14-in. rope. Braid ropes. Center 14-in. braid on top of the shorter braid. Pinch ends to seal and tuck under. Cover and let rise until doubled, about 30 minutes.

Beat egg and water; brush over dough. Sprinkle with poppy seeds. Bake at 375° for 25-30 minutes or until golden brown. Cover with foil during the last 15 minutes of baking. Remove from pan to cool on a wire rack. **Yield:** 1 loaf.

GOLDEN PUMPKIN ROLLS
Kathy Anderson, Lexington, Kentucky

My grandmother gave me the recipe for these rolls years ago. Best served warm, they complement any holiday menu.

      2 packages (1/4 ounce *each*) active dry yeast
    1/2 cup warm water (110° to 115°)
    1/2 teaspoon sugar
    3/4 cup warm milk (110° to 115°)
    1/2 cup packed brown sugar
    1/2 cup cooked *or* canned pumpkin
      3 tablespoons butter *or* margarine, melted
      1 teaspoon salt
    1/2 teaspoon ground ginger
    1/4 to 1/2 teaspoon ground nutmeg
    1/4 to 1/2 teaspoon ground cloves
      4 to 4-1/2 cups all-purpose flour

In a mixing bowl, dissolve yeast in warm water. Sprinkle with sugar; let stand for 5 minutes. Add milk, brown sugar, pumpkin, butter, salt, spices and 2 cups flour; beat until smooth. Stir in enough remaining flour to form a soft dough.

Turn onto a floured surface; knead until smooth and elastic, about 6-8 minutes. Place in a greased bowl, turning once to grease top. Cover and let rise in a warm place until doubled, about 1 hour. Punch dough down. Turn onto a floured surface; divide into 24 pieces. Shape each into a roll. Place 2 in. apart on greased baking sheets. Bake at 350° for 15-20 minutes. **Yield:** 2 dozen.

Editor's Note: Dough may be shaped into two loaves and baked in greased 9-in. x 5-in. x 3-in. pans for 25-30 minutes.

LEMON CHIP MUFFINS
Maria Bremer, McHenry, Illinois

The mellow flavor of these chocolate chip muffins is enhanced by a sweet lemony topping. They're just right for a ladies' luncheon.

    1/2 cup butter *or* margarine, softened
      1 cup plus 2 tablespoons sugar, *divided*
      2 eggs
      2 cups all-purpose flour
      1 teaspoon baking soda
      1 cup buttermilk *or* plain yogurt
    3/4 cup miniature semisweet chocolate chips
      1 tablespoon grated lemon peel
    1/4 cup lemon juice

In a mixing bowl, cream butter and 1 cup sugar. Add eggs, one at a time, beating well after each addition. Combine flour and baking soda; add to the creamed mixture alternately with buttermilk. Fold in chocolate chips and lemon peel. Fill paper-lined muffin cups two-thirds full.

Bake at 375° for 18-20 minutes or until a toothpick comes out clean. Brush tops with lemon juice; sprinkle with remaining sugar. Cool for 5 minutes before removing from pans to wire racks. Serve warm. **Yield:** 1-1/2 dozen.

PLUM COFFEE LOAF
Janet Snider, Kalamazoo, Michigan

I've baked this moist bread for so long that I don't recall where I got the recipe. A simple-to-make plum filling and hot roll mix make it easy to whip up on Christmas morning.

    1 package (16 ounces) hot roll mix
    2 tablespoons butter *or* margarine, melted
    1 can (30 ounces) purple plums, drained, halved
       and pitted
    1/4 cup sugar
    1/4 teaspoon ground cinnamon
    1/8 teaspoon ground cloves
GLAZE:
    1 cup confectioners' sugar
    1/4 to 1/2 teaspoon almond extract
    1 to 2 tablespoons milk
    1/3 cup slivered almonds

Prepare and knead hot roll mix according to package directions. Place in a greased bowl, turning once to grease top. Cover and let rise in a warm place until doubled, about 30 minutes. Punch dough down. Turn onto a lightly floured surface; roll into a 15-in. x 10-in. rectangle. Brush with butter.

Place plums, cut side down, lengthwise down the center third of rectangle. Combine sugar, cinnamon and cloves; sprinkle over plums. Fold both long sides of dough over filling; pinch seam to seal and tuck ends under. Carefully transfer to a greased baking sheet (dough will be very soft). With a sharp knife, make slashes 1 in. apart across top of loaf. Cover and let rise until doubled, about 30 minutes.

Bake at 350° for 20-25 minutes or until golden brown. Remove from pan to a wire rack to cool. For glaze, combine confectioners' sugar, extract and enough milk to achieve desired consistency. Drizzle over warm loaf. Sprinkle with almonds. **Yield:** 1 loaf.

CREAM CHEESE PINWHEELS
Naticia Lethbridge, Eckville, Alberta

These eye-catching pinwheels always bake up beautifully. The sweetened cream cheese filling is rich and satisfying.

2-3/4 to 3-1/4 cups all-purpose flour
    1/3 cup sugar
    1 package (1/4 ounce) quick-rise yeast
    1 teaspoon grated lemon peel
    1/2 teaspoon salt
    1/2 cup milk
    1/3 cup butter *or* margarine, softened
    1/4 cup water
    1 egg
    1 egg white

FILLING:
    1 package (8 ounces) cream cheese, softened
    1/4 cup sugar
    1 tablespoon lemon juice
EGG WASH:
    1 egg white
    1 teaspoon water
    1 tablespoon sugar

In a mixing bowl, combine 2 cups flour, sugar, yeast, lemon peel and salt. In a saucepan, heat milk, butter and water to 120°-130°. Add to dry ingredients; beat until moistened. Add egg and egg white; beat on medium speed for 2 minutes. Stir in enough remaining flour to form a soft dough. Cover and let rest for 10 minutes. Turn onto a lightly floured surface. Roll into a 12-in. square; cut into sixteen 3-in. squares.

Combine filling ingredients; spoon onto center of each square. To form pinwheels, diagonally cut dough from each corner to within 3/4 in. of the center. Fold every other point toward the center, overlapping pieces. Moisten center edges with water; pinch to seal. Place 3 in. apart on greased baking sheets. Cover and let rise in a warm place until doubled, about 45 minutes.

Beat egg white and water; brush over pinwheels. Sprinkle with sugar. Bake at 350° for 15-20 minutes or until lightly browned. Remove from pans to cool on wire racks. **Yield:** 16 rolls.

SWEET SAUSAGE COFFEE RING
Jenny Nichols, Arlington, Texas

I came across this recipe one year while judging at our county fair. It's a hearty bread that's well suited for colder weather.

    1 cup water
    1 cup golden raisins
    1 pound bulk pork sausage
1-1/2 cups sugar
1-1/2 cups packed brown sugar
    2 eggs
    1 cup chopped pecans
    3 cups all-purpose flour
    1 teaspoon baking powder
    1 teaspoon baking soda
    1 teaspoon ground ginger
    1 teaspoon pumpkin pie spice
    1 cup strong brewed coffee, room temperature
GLAZE:
    1/2 cup confectioners' sugar
    2 teaspoons milk
    1/4 teaspoon vanilla extract

In a saucepan, bring water to a boil; reduce heat. Add raisins. Cover and simmer for 5 minutes; drain and set aside. Crumble sausage into a large bowl. Add sugars and eggs; mix well. Stir in pecans and reserved raisins. Combine the flour, baking powder, baking soda, ginger and pie spice; add to sausage mixture alternately with coffee.

Transfer to a greased and floured 10-in. tube pan. Bake at 350° for 1-1/4 to 1-1/2 hours or until a toothpick inserted near the center comes out clean. Cool for 10 minutes before removing from pan to a wire rack. Combine glaze ingredients; drizzle over cooled bread. Refrigerate leftovers. **Yield:** 12-16 servings.

SAVORY APPETIZERS. Shown clockwise from top: Crisp Cheese Twists (p. 21), Festive Vegetable Dip (p. 21) and Zesty Marinated Shrimp (p. 21).

Appetizers

CRISP CHEESE TWISTS
Kelly-Ann Gibbons, Prince George, British Columbia
(Pictured on page 20)

These golden twists are always popular. We like them along-side chili and soup. My husband and daughter usually try to sneak a few from the cooling rack when I make them.

1-1/4 cups all-purpose flour
1/2 cup cornmeal
1 teaspoon salt
1/4 cup shortening
1-1/4 cups shredded cheddar cheese
1/3 cup cold water
Grated Parmesan cheese

In a large bowl, combine the flour, cornmeal and salt. Cut in shortening until mixture resembles coarse crumbs. Stir in cheddar cheese. Sprinkle with 1/3 cup water. Toss with a fork (if dough is dry, add water, 1 teaspoon at a time, until dough forms a ball). Wrap tightly in plastic wrap; refrigerate for 1 hour or until firm.
Divide dough in half. On a lightly floured surface, roll each portion into an 11-in. x 10-in. rectangle. Cut into 5-in. x 1/2-in. strips. Carefully twist each strip and place on greased baking sheets, pressing ends down.
Bake at 425° for 7-9 minutes or until golden brown. Immediately sprinkle twists with Parmesan cheese. Cool on wire racks. Store in an airtight container. **Yield:** about 7 dozen.

FESTIVE VEGETABLE DIP
Mary Pollard, Crossville, Tennessee
(Pictured on page 20)

I like to serve this well-seasoned dip with veggies. It rounds out a holiday snack buffet in a festive way when it's served in hollowed-out green and red bell peppers.

1 cup mayonnaise
1/2 cup sour cream
2 tablespoons minced fresh parsley
1 tablespoon minced chives
1 teaspoon dried minced onion
1/2 teaspoon lemon juice
1/2 teaspoon Worcestershire sauce
1/4 teaspoon salt
1/4 teaspoon paprika
1/8 teaspoon curry powder
1/8 teaspoon pepper
1 medium green pepper
1 medium sweet red pepper
Assorted raw vegetables

In a large bowl, combine the first 11 ingredients. Cover and refrigerate for at least 1 hour. Lay green pepper on its side; with a sharp knife, make a horizontal slice just above stem. Remove top piece; save for another use. Remove membrane and seeds. Repeat with red pepper. Fill peppers with dip. Serve with vegetables. **Yield:** 1-1/2 cups.

ZESTY MARINATED SHRIMP
Mary Jane Guest, Alamosa, Colorado
(Pictured on page 20)

These easy shrimp look impressive on a buffet table and taste even better! The zesty sauce has a wonderful spicy cit-rus flavor. I especially like this recipe because I can prepare it ahead of time.

1/2 cup vegetable oil
1/2 cup lime juice
1/2 cup thinly sliced red onion
6 lemon slices
1 tablespoon minced fresh parsley
1/2 teaspoon salt
1/2 teaspoon dill weed
1/8 teaspoon hot pepper sauce
2 pounds medium shrimp, cooked, peeled and deveined

In a large bowl, combine the first eight ingredients. Stir in shrimp. Cover and refrigerate for 4 hours, stirring occasionally. Drain before serving. **Yield:** 12 servings.

SOUTHWESTERN APPETIZER TRIANGLES
Sheila Pope, Preston, Idaho

A nifty cross between egg rolls and tacos, these triangles are fun to serve, especially at the holidays. My mom created the recipe years ago, much to the delight of my family. Since I began making them, my husband insists we have them on Sundays during football season as well as for holiday celebrations.

1 pound ground beef
1 medium onion, chopped
Salt and pepper to taste
1 can (16 ounces) refried beans
1-1/2 cups (6 ounces) shredded cheddar cheese
1 cup salsa
1 can (4 ounces) diced jalapeno peppers, drained
2 packages (12 ounces *each*) wonton wrappers*
Oil for deep-fat frying
Additional salsa

In a skillet over medium heat, cook beef, onion, salt and pepper until meat is no longer pink; drain. Add the beans, cheese, salsa and jalapenos. Cook and stir over low heat until the cheese is melted. Remove from the heat; cool for 10 minutes.
Place a teaspoonful of beef mixture in the center of one wonton wrapper. Moisten edges with water. Fold wontons in half, forming a triangle. Repeat. In an electric skillet or deep-fat fryer, heat 1 in. of oil to 375°. Fry wontons, a few at a time, for 2-3 minutes or until golden brown. Drain on paper towels. Serve warm with salsa. **Yield:** about 7-1/2 dozen.
*Editor's Note: Fill wonton wrappers a few at a time, keeping others covered until ready to use.

HOLIDAY PARTY DEVILED EGGS
Edie DeSpain, Logan, Utah

My family's enjoyed these tidbits for many years and for good reason—the eggs are just delicious. What's the secret? I add cream cheese to the filling to make it smooth and rich.

- 10 hard-cooked eggs
- 1 package (3 ounces) cream cheese, softened
- 1/4 cup mayonnaise
- 1 teaspoon prepared mustard
- 1/8 teaspoon Worcestershire sauce
- 1/8 teaspoon salt
- Dash white pepper
- Paprika, pimientos and fresh parsley

Slice eggs in half lengthwise; remove yolks and set whites aside. In a small bowl, mash yolks with a fork. Add the cream cheese, mayonnaise, mustard, Worcestershire sauce, salt and pepper; mix well. Stuff or pipe filling into egg whites. Garnish with paprika, pimientos and parsley. **Yield:** 20 servings.

DATE SNACK CRACKERS
Nettie Vandy, Lexington, Kentucky

These delicious tidbits add a sweet element to a holiday lineup. The dates and nuts taste wonderful topped with fluffy frosting. And since the two toppings can be stored separately in the fridge, you don't have to make them all at once.

- 1 can (14 ounces) sweetened condensed milk
- 1-1/2 cups chopped dates
- 1-1/2 cups chopped walnuts
- 1 package (10 ounces) butter-flavored crackers
- 2 packages (3 ounces *each*) cream cheese, softened
- 2-1/2 cups confectioners' sugar
- 1/2 teaspoon vanilla or coconut extract

In a bowl, combine the milk, dates and walnuts. Cover and refrigerate for 3 hours or until firm. Spread level teaspoonfuls on each cracker. Place crackers on greased baking sheets. Bake at 350° for 8-10 minutes. Remove to wire racks to cool.

For frosting, beat cream cheese in a mixing bowl. Gradually add sugar and vanilla; beat until smooth. Spread over crackers. Store in the refrigerator. **Yield:** about 8 dozen.

NUTTY STUFFED MUSHROOMS
Mildred Eldred, Union City, Michigan

Basil, Parmesan cheese and mushrooms blend together well, while buttery pecans give these treats a surprising crunch. Our children, grandchildren and great-grandchildren always ask for them!

- 18 to 20 large fresh mushrooms
- 1 small onion, chopped
- 3 tablespoons butter *or* margarine
- 1/4 cup dry bread crumbs
- 1/4 cup finely chopped pecans
- 3 tablespoons grated Parmesan cheese
- 1/4 teaspoon salt
- 1/4 teaspoon dried basil
- Dash cayenne pepper

Remove stems from mushrooms; set caps aside. Finely chop stems; place in a paper towel and squeeze to remove any liquid. In a skillet, saute chopped mushrooms and onion in butter for 5 minutes or until tender. Remove from the heat; set aside.

In a small bowl, combine the bread crumbs, pecans, Parmesan cheese, salt, basil and pepper; add mushroom mixture. Stuff firmly into mushroom caps. Place in a greased 15-in. x 10-in. x 1-in. baking pan. Bake, uncovered, at 400° for 15-18 minutes or until tender. Serve hot. **Yield:** 18-20 servings.

COCONUT CHICKEN BITES
Linda Schwarz, Bertrand, Nebraska

These tender nuggets are great for nibbling, thanks to the coconut, cumin, celery salt and garlic powder that season them. I've served the bites several times for parties, and everyone enjoyed them.

- 2 cups flaked coconut
- 1 egg
- 2 tablespoons milk
- 3/4 pound boneless skinless chicken breasts, cut into 3/4-inch pieces
- 1/2 cup all-purpose flour
- Oil for deep-fat frying
- 1 teaspoon celery salt
- 1/2 teaspoon garlic powder
- 1/2 teaspoon ground cumin

In a blender or food processor, process coconut until finely chopped. Transfer to a bowl and set aside. In another bowl, combine egg and milk. Toss chicken with flour; dip in egg mixture, then in coconut. Place in a single layer on a baking sheet. Refrigerate for 30 minutes.

In an electric skillet or deep-fat fryer, heat 2 in. of oil to 375°. Fry chicken, a few pieces at a time, for 1-1/2 minutes on each side or until golden brown. Drain on paper towels; place in a bowl. Sprinkle with celery salt, garlic powder and cumin; toss to coat. Serve warm. **Yield:** about 3 dozen.

CURRIED CHUTNEY CHEESE SPREAD
Leslie Suffich, Mobile, Alabama

It's impossible to stop eating this distinctive spread once you start. I like it because it's an eye-catching dish to serve, and it has an intriguing blend of flavors and textures. People have fun guessing the ingredients.

- 2 packages (8 ounces *each*) cream cheese, cubed
- 2 cups (8 ounces) shredded cheddar cheese
- 1/3 cup apple juice
- 2 tablespoons Worcestershire sauce
- 2 teaspoons vanilla extract
- 1 teaspoon curry powder
- 1/2 teaspoon salt
- 1 jar (9 ounces) mango chutney

1/2 cup chopped green onions
1/2 cup flaked coconut
1/2 cup finely chopped unsalted peanuts
Assorted crackers

In a blender or food processor, combine the first seven ingredients. Cover and process until smooth. Spread into a 1/2-in.-thick circle on a 10-in. serving plate. Cover and refrigerate. Just before serving, spread chutney over cheese mixture. Sprinkle with onions, coconut and peanuts. Serve with crackers. **Yield:** about 5 cups.

HAMMETTES
Marguerite Jensen, Rockford, Illinois

With the flavor of roasted ham in bite-sized morsels, these hammettes are a nice change from traditional party meatballs. They're a popular snack that appeals to most palates.

2 eggs
1 cup milk
2 cups dry bread crumbs
1-1/2 pounds ground fully cooked ham (6 cups)
1 pound ground pork
1 cup packed brown sugar
1/2 cup vinegar
1/2 cup pineapple juice
1 teaspoon ground mustard
6 whole cloves

In a bowl, beat eggs and milk. Add the bread crumbs, ham and pork; mix well. Using about 3 tablespoons for each, shape mixture into logs. Place in a lightly greased 15-in. x 10-in. x 1-in. baking pan. Bake, uncovered, at 350° for 30 minutes.

Meanwhile, in a saucepan, bring the brown sugar, vinegar, pineapple juice, mustard and cloves to a boil. Pour over logs. Cover and bake at 350° for 1-1/4 hours, basting occasionally with sauce. Uncover and bake 15 minutes longer. Discard cloves. Serve warm. **Yield:** about 3-1/2 dozen.

CRUNCHY COMBO
Gloria Schmitz, Elkhart, Indiana

My husband and our four sons enjoy this mix any time of year. I love to munch on it while wrapping holiday gifts. What's more, the snack carries well to gatherings and makes a nice present when packaged in pretty tins.

6 cups toasted oat cereal*
1-1/2 cups miniature pretzels
1-1/2 cups Cheetos
1/2 cup butter *or* margarine, melted
1/4 cup grated Parmesan cheese
1/2 teaspoon garlic salt
1/2 teaspoon onion salt
1/2 teaspoon Italian seasoning, optional

In a large bowl, combine the cereal, pretzels and Cheetos. Combine the remaining ingredients; pour over cereal mixture and stir to coat. Spread into an ungreased 15-in.

x 10-in. x 1-in. baking pan. Bake at 275° for 30 minutes, stirring every 10 minutes. Cool. Store in an airtight container. **Yield:** about 9 cups.

*Editor's Note: This recipe was tested with Quaker Toasted Oatmeal Squares.

CREAMY SHRIMP MOUSSE
Eloise Bingenheimer, Salem, Oregon

Folks will think you're spoiling them when you serve this wonderful shrimp mousse! Molded in a ring, it looks fancy even as it feeds a crowd.

1 can (10-3/4 ounces) condensed cream of mushroom soup, undiluted
1 package (8 ounces) cream cheese, cubed
1 cup mayonnaise
1 envelope unflavored gelatin
6 tablespoons cold water
1 can (6 ounces) small shrimp, rinsed and drained *or* 1/3 cup frozen small cooked shrimp, thawed
3/4 cup chopped onion
1/2 cup chopped celery
Lettuce leaves
Fresh parsley, optional
Assorted crackers

In a saucepan, combine the soup, cream cheese and mayonnaise. Cook and stir over medium heat until smooth; remove from the heat. In a small saucepan, sprinkle the gelatin over water; let stand for 1 minute. Heat on low until the gelatin is dissolved. Transfer to a mixing bowl; cool slightly.

Add the shrimp, onion, celery and cream cheese mixture. Transfer to a lightly greased 6-cup mold. Cover and refrigerate for 4 hours or overnight. Unmold onto a lettuce-lined serving plate. Garnish with parsley if desired. Serve with crackers. Refrigerate leftovers. **Yield:** 5 cups.

HOT PARMESAN PUFFS
Patricia Brewer, Clanton, Alabama

These scrumptious puffs come from the oven golden brown and bubbly. I make them often to serve at parties. For a change of pace, I'll use Swiss cheese instead of Parmesan.

16 slices bread
1 cup mayonnaise
1 package (3 ounces) cream cheese, softened
1/3 cup grated Parmesan cheese
2 teaspoons grated onion
1/8 teaspoon cayenne pepper
Additional Parmesan cheese

Using a 2-in. round or diamond cookie cutter, cut shapes from bread slices. Place on ungreased baking sheets. Bake at 300° for 8-10 minutes or until toasted.

Meanwhile, in a small mixing bowl, combine the mayonnaise, cream cheese, Parmesan cheese, onion and cayenne. Spread on bread. Sprinkle with additional Parmesan. Broil 4 in. from the heat for 2-3 minutes or until golden brown and bubbly. Serve warm. **Yield:** about 3 dozen.

Christmas Dinner

ORANGE-GLAZED CORNISH HENS
Mary Jo Hopkins, Hobart, Indiana
(Pictured below)

One year, I served this recipe and got nothing but raves. My family prefers these moist glazed hens instead of turkey.

    1 cup finely chopped onion
    1 cup finely chopped celery
    1/2 cup sliced almonds
    1/2 cup butter *or* margarine
    3 cups cooked rice
    4 teaspoons sugar
    1 teaspoon salt
    1/2 teaspoon dried thyme
    1/4 cup grated orange peel
    4 Cornish game hens (about 20 ounces *each*)
GLAZE:
    1 cup orange juice
    1/4 cup honey
    1/4 cup vegetable oil
    1 tablespoon grated orange peel

In a skillet, saute the onion, celery and almonds in butter. Add rice, sugar, salt, thyme and orange peel; mix well. Loosely stuff hens. Place, breast side up, on a rack in a shallow baking pan. In a small bowl, combine glaze ingredients; spoon some over hens. Bake, uncovered, at 350° for 40 minutes. Cover and bake 40 minutes longer until juices run clear, brushing often with remaining glaze. **Yield:** 4 servings.

PORK LOIN SUPPER
Lois McAtee, Oceanside, California
(Pictured on page 26)

A hint of cinnamon gives additional flavor to this tender roast, while the vegetables and dried fruits add extra goodness. This recipe was given to me by my aunt over 30 years ago. It's a complete meal in one pan.

    1 teaspoon salt
    1 teaspoon pepper
    1 teaspoon garlic powder
    1 teaspoon paprika
    1 bone-in pork loin roast (about 4-1/2 pounds)
    6 medium potatoes, peeled and cut into 1-inch
      pieces
    6 medium carrots, cut into 1/2-inch pieces
   12 pitted prunes
   12 dried apricots
    1 thin lemon slice
    2 cans (10-1/2 ounces *each*) condensed beef
      broth, undiluted
    1/4 cup butter *or* margarine, melted
    1/2 teaspoon ground cinnamon

Combine salt, pepper, garlic powder and paprika; rub over the roast. Place in a shallow roasting pan. Arrange vegetables and fruit around roast. Combine broth, butter and cinnamon; pour over vegetable mixture. Cover and bake at 350° for 45 minutes. Uncover; bake 1-1/2 hours longer or until a meat thermometer reads 160°, basting often. Cover and let stand for 10 minutes before carving. **Yield:** 8-10 servings.

CORNMEAL PARKERHOUSE ROLLS
Lisa Darnall Lapaseotes, Bridgeport, Nebraska
(Pictured on page 27)

My mom deserves the credit for making this recipe a family tradition. These sweet tender rolls have been on every holiday table at her house for as long as I can remember.

    1/2 cup butter *or* margarine
    1/2 cup sugar
    1/3 cup cornmeal
    1 teaspoon salt
    2 cups milk
    1 package (1/4 ounce) active dry yeast
    1/2 cup warm water (110° to 115°)
    2 eggs
4-1/2 to 5-1/2 cups all-purpose flour
Melted butter *or* margarine

In a saucepan, melt butter. Stir in the sugar, cornmeal and salt. Gradually add milk. Bring to a boil over medium-high heat, stirring constantly. Reduce heat; cook and stir for 5-10 minutes or until thickened. Cool to 110°-115°. In a mixing bowl, dissolve yeast in warm water. Add eggs and cornmeal mixture. Beat in enough flour to form a soft dough.

Turn onto a floured surface; knead until smooth and elastic, about 6-8 minutes. Place in a greased bowl, turning once to grease top. Cover and let rise in a warm place until doubled, about 1 hour.

Punch dough down. Turn onto a lightly floured surface; roll out to 1/2-in. thickness. Cut with a floured 2-1/2-in. biscuit cutter. Brush with melted butter; fold in half. Place 2 in. apart on greased baking sheets. Cover and let rise until nearly doubled, about 30 minutes. Bake at 375° for 15-20 minutes or until golden brown. Brush with butter. Remove from pans to cool on wire racks. **Yield:** 2-3 dozen.

LEMON-DILLED BRUSSELS SPROUTS
Marlyn Duff, New Berlin, Wisconsin
(Pictured on page 27)

Brussels sprouts get dressed up for the holidays when I make this flavorful dish. Lemon and dill season the buttery sauce, and chopped walnuts add just the right crunch.

```
1-1/2 pounds fresh brussels sprouts
  1/3 cup butter or margarine
    2 tablespoons lemon juice
    1 teaspoon dill weed
  1/2 teaspoon salt
  1/8 teaspoon pepper
    2 tablespoons finely chopped walnuts
```

In a saucepan, bring brussels sprouts and 1 in. of water to a boil. Reduce heat; cover and simmer for 8-10 minutes or until tender. Meanwhile, in another saucepan, melt butter. Stir in the lemon juice, dill, salt and pepper; cook and stir for 1 minute. Drain sprouts; add to butter mixture and toss to coat. Sprinkle with walnuts. **Yield:** 4-6 servings.

WHITE CHOCOLATE PUDDING
Elizabeth Olds-Barrett, East Haven, Connecticut
(Pictured on pages 26 and 27)

I adapted a milk chocolate pudding recipe to suit my preference for white chocolate. Made from scratch, this delicious treat has wonderful homemade goodness. My family requests it often.

```
1/2 cup sugar
  3 tablespoons cornstarch
1/8 teaspoon salt
  2 cups whipping cream
  2 cups milk
  6 egg yolks, lightly beaten
3/4 cup vanilla or white chips
  1 teaspoon orange or rum extract
```

In a heavy saucepan, combine sugar, cornstarch and salt. Gradually add cream and milk. Bring to a boil over medium-high heat, stirring constantly. Reduce heat; cook and stir with a wire whisk 2-3 minutes more or until thickened. Remove from the heat. Stir 1-1/2 cups hot mixture into egg yolks; return to saucepan. Stirring constantly, bring to a gentle boil; cook and stir 2 minutes more. Remove from the heat; stir in chips until melted. Stir in extract. **Yield:** 8 servings.

ITALIAN SALAD
Sandy Moran, Manteno, Illinois

This salad's easy since the dressing is made ahead. What's more, it's proved popular with everyone who tastes it.

```
    1 cup olive or vegetable oil
    6 tablespoons red wine vinegar or cider vinegar
    1 jar (4 ounces) diced pimientos, drained
    1 garlic clove, minced
  1/3 cup grated Parmesan cheese
  1/2 teaspoon salt
  1/4 teaspoon pepper
    1 can (14 ounces) artichoke hearts, drained and
        quartered
    1 medium red onion, halved and sliced
   16 to 18 cups torn salad greens
Additional Parmesan cheese, optional
```

In a jar with a tight-fitting lid, combine the first seven ingredients; shake well. In a bowl, combine artichokes and onion. Add dressing and toss gently. Cover and refrigerate for at least 8 hours. Just before serving, pour artichoke mixture over greens and toss to coat. Sprinkle with additional Parmesan if desired. **Yield:** 14-16 servings.

SIRLOIN WITH SOUR CREAM SAUCE
Kim Schmitt, Bellingham, Washington

My in-laws raise beef for all their children, so I'm always looking for new ways to cook steak. This is an absolute favorite. It's so easy to fix, and the result is a tender steak smothered in a creamy onion and mushroom sauce. The aroma alone makes my husband's mouth water!

```
    3 tablespoons all-purpose flour, divided
  1/2 teaspoon salt
  1/2 teaspoon pepper
  1/2 teaspoon paprika
1-1/2 pounds boneless beef sirloin steak, cut into
        serving-size pieces
    2 tablespoons vegetable oil
  1/2 cup chopped onion
    2 cups sliced fresh mushrooms
    1 garlic clove, minced
  2/3 cup water, divided
    2 tablespoons brown sugar
    2 tablespoons soy sauce
    1 teaspoon Dijon mustard
  1/2 cup sour cream
Hot cooked noodles or rice
```

In a large resealable plastic bag, combine 2 tablespoons flour, salt, pepper and paprika; add beef and toss to coat. In a skillet, brown beef on all sides in oil. Add the onion, mushrooms, garlic, 1/2 cup water, brown sugar, soy sauce and mustard; cover and simmer for 10-15 minutes or until meat is tender. Remove meat to a serving platter and keep warm.

Combine remaining flour and water until smooth; stir into skillet. Bring to a boil; cook and stir for 2 minutes or until thickened. Reduce heat; stir in sour cream. Heat gently (do not boil). Serve beef and sauce over noodles. **Yield:** 4-6 servings.

FESTIVE FEAST. Shown clockwise from top right: Cornmeal Parkerhouse Rolls (p. 24), Lemon-Dilled Brussels Sprouts (p. 25), Pork Loin Supper (p. 24) and White Chocolate Pudding (p. 25).

CINNAMON APPLE CRISP
Verna Hofer, Mitchell, South Dakota

One of the desserts I always make when everyone comes home for Christmas is this scrumptious crisp. We enjoy the brown sugar, cinnamon, walnut and graham cracker topping better than the traditional oat-topped version.

    10 cups sliced peeled tart apples
    1/2 cup sugar
    1/4 cup red-hot candies
    1/2 cup boiling water
1-1/2 cups graham cracker crumbs (about 24 squares)
    1/2 cup all-purpose flour
    1/2 cup packed brown sugar
    1/2 cup chopped walnuts
      1 teaspoon ground cinnamon
    1/2 cup cold butter *or* margarine

Place apples in a greased 13-in. x 9-in. x 2-in. baking dish. Sprinkle with sugar and red-hots. Pour water over apples. In a bowl, combine the cracker crumbs, flour, brown sugar, walnuts and cinnamon; cut in butter until crumbly. Sprinkle over apple mixture. Bake, uncovered, at 325° for 50-55 minutes or until apples are tender. **Yield:** 12-16 servings.

CRANBERRY RICE PILAF
S. Sonnon, Peru, Illinois

This deliciously different pilaf gets its festive color from tart cranberries, while brown rice provides wholesome flavor. It's excellent alongside poultry.

      1 cup chicken broth
    1/2 cup orange juice
      2 tablespoons sugar
1-1/2 cups uncooked instant brown rice
    1/2 cup fresh *or* frozen cranberries, thawed
      1 tablespoon butter *or* margarine
      2 tablespoons sliced almonds, toasted

In a saucepan, bring the broth, orange juice and sugar to a boil. Stir in the rice, cranberries and butter. Reduce heat; cover and cook for 5-8 minutes or until water is absorbed. Remove from the heat and let stand for 5 minutes. Sprinkle with almonds. **Yield:** 4 servings.

CAULIFLOWER AU GRATIN
Kathryn Herman, Villisca, Iowa

The first time I made this rich side dish for a big family meal, it was an instant hit. When everyone had eaten their fill, there was a lively discussion on who would be the lucky one to take home the leftovers!

      1 medium head cauliflower (about 1-1/2 pounds),
        broken into florets
      2 garlic cloves, minced
      6 tablespoons butter *or* margarine
      2 tablespoons all-purpose flour
1-1/2 cups milk
      4 bacon strips, cooked and crumbled
    1/4 teaspoon salt
    1/8 teaspoon pepper
Dash cayenne pepper
      1 cup (4 ounces) shredded Swiss cheese

In a large saucepan, bring cauliflower and 1 in. of water to a boil. Reduce heat; cover and cook for 6-7 minutes or until crisp-tender. Drain well; set aside. In another saucepan, saute garlic in butter for 1 minute. Stir in flour until blended; gradually add milk. Bring to a boil; cook and stir for 2 minutes or until thickened.

Remove from the heat; stir in cauliflower, bacon, salt, pepper and cayenne. Pour into a greased 1-1/2-qt. baking dish. Sprinkle with cheese. Bake, uncovered, at 400° for 15-20 minutes or until cheese is melted. **Yield:** 5-7 servings.

SWEET POTATO BISCUITS
Marjorie Webster, Madison Heights, Virginia

Moist and sweet, these biscuits are a delightful addition to any holiday meal—even breakfast. They don't need butter...but they'll taste even better when you spread some on.

3-1/2 cups all-purpose flour
4-1/2 teaspoons baking powder
      1 teaspoon salt
    1/2 teaspoon ground cinnamon
1-1/2 cups mashed cooked sweet potatoes (prepared
        without milk or butter)
    1/2 cup butter *or* margarine, melted
    1/2 cup sugar
      2 tablespoons milk

In a large mixing bowl, combine the flour, baking powder, salt and cinnamon. In another bowl, combine sweet potatoes, butter, sugar and milk; add to flour mixture and mix well. Turn onto a floured surface; knead 8-10 times. Roll to 1/2-in. thickness. Cut with a 2-1/2-in. biscuit cutter; place on greased baking sheet. Bake at 400° for 15-18 minutes or until golden brown. **Yield:** about 1-1/2 dozen.

GOLDEN SQUASH BAKE
Mary McKay, Sault Saint Marie, Ontario

I save this memorable casserole for the holidays. We all look forward to it! The squash has a slight tang from sour cream, and allspice lends delightful aroma and flavor.

    1/2 cup chopped onion
      2 tablespoons butter *or* margarine
      3 cups cooked mashed winter squash
      1 cup (8 ounces) sour cream
      1 teaspoon salt
    1/4 to 1/2 teaspoon ground allspice
    1/4 teaspoon pepper
      1 tablespoon grated Parmesan cheese

In a skillet, saute onion in butter until tender. Remove from the heat. Stir in squash, sour cream, salt, allspice and pepper. Transfer to a greased 1-qt. baking dish; sprinkle with Parmesan cheese. Bake, uncovered, at 375° for 25-30 minutes. **Yield:** 6-8 servings.

CHRISTMAS SEAFOOD SOUP
Sue Bridley, Dennison, Minnesota

For as long as I can remember, we always had this wonderful soup on Christmas Day. In our part of the country, where winters are long and cold, this sure warms us up.

2 cans (6-1/2 ounces *each*) chopped clams
2 cups diced peeled potatoes
2 cups chopped celery
2 cups diced carrots
1/2 cup water
2 cups milk
1 package (5 ounces) frozen cooked shrimp, thawed
4 bacon strips, cooked and crumbled
2 teaspoons minced fresh parsley
Salt and pepper to taste

Drain the clams, reserving juice; set clams aside. In a large saucepan or Dutch oven, combine clam juice, potatoes, celery, carrots and water. Bring to a boil. Reduce heat; cover and cook for 15 minutes or until vegetables are tender. Add the milk, shrimp, bacon, parsley, salt, pepper and reserved clams; heat through. **Yield:** 7 servings.

SPINACH POTATOES
Adele Brooks, La Palma, California

This potato dish is considered a special treat even by my grandchildren and great-grandchildren. It came to me from a dear friend who was raised on a farm in Kansas, and it's one of my personal favorites. The creamy spuds, spinach and melted cheese provide down-home flavor that can't be beat. It's a great side to bring to a potluck.

6 to 8 potatoes, peeled and diced
3/4 cup sour cream
1/2 cup butter *or* margarine, melted
2 tablespoons sugar
2 teaspoons salt
1/4 teaspoon pepper
1 package (10 ounces) frozen chopped spinach, cooked and drained
2 tablespoons minced chives
1-1/4 teaspoons dill weed
1 cup (4 ounces) shredded cheddar cheese

In a bowl, combine the potatoes, sour cream, butter, sugar, salt and pepper. Add the spinach, chives and dill. Spoon into a greased 2-qt. baking dish. Sprinkle with cheese. Bake, uncovered, at 400° for 20 minutes or until heated through. **Yield:** 8-10 servings.

MUSHROOM BARLEY BAKE
Jean Simons, Winnipeg, Manitoba

The first time I tasted this barley bake was when my daughter, a busy nurse, mother and farm wife, made it one night. Its tempting flavor prompted the whole family to ask for seconds.

3/4 pound fresh mushrooms, sliced
2 medium onions, chopped

1/4 cup butter *or* margarine
1-1/2 cups pearl barley
1 jar (2 ounces) diced pimientos, drained
6 teaspoons chicken bouillon, *divided*
4 cups boiling water, *divided*

In a skillet, saute mushrooms and onions in butter until tender. Stir in barley and pimientos. Transfer to a greased 13-in. x 9-in. x 2-in. baking dish. Dissolve 3 teaspoons bouillon in 2 cups water; stir into barley mixture. Cover and bake at 325° for 1 hour. Dissolve remaining bouillon in remaining water; stir into barley mixture. Bake, uncovered, 30 minutes longer or until liquid is absorbed and barley is tender. **Yield:** 8-10 servings.

GLAZED DIJON CARROTS
Teri Lindquist, Gurnee, Illinois

I not only serve these sweet glazed carrots during the holidays, but many times throughout the year as well. Not only is it delightfully different, it tastes so good all the kids gladly gobble it up!

1 package (16 ounces) baby carrots
1/2 cup water
3 tablespoons butter *or* margarine
2 tablespoons brown sugar
1 tablespoon Dijon mustard
1/2 teaspoon ground ginger
1/4 teaspoon salt

In a saucepan, bring carrots and water to a boil. Reduce heat; cover and cook for 10-12 minutes or until tender. Drain. Place carrots in a serving dish and keep warm. In the same pan, melt butter. Add brown sugar, mustard, ginger and salt; cook and stir over medium heat until sugar is dissolved. Pour over carrots and toss to coat. **Yield:** 4-6 servings.

COLORFUL COLESLAW
Audrey Thibodeau, Mesa, Arizona

We enjoy the interesting blend of flavors and textures in this crisp cabbage slaw. It adds nice color and refreshing crunch to our Christmas feast.

3 cups shredded green cabbage
3 cups shredded red cabbage
3 tablespoons minced fresh parsley
1 carton (8 ounces) lemon yogurt
1 tablespoon sugar
1 tablespoon lemon juice
1 teaspoon ground mustard
1/4 teaspoon salt
1/4 teaspoon pepper
1 cup halved seedless red grapes
1/4 cup slivered almonds, toasted
1 teaspoon sesame seeds

In a bowl, combine cabbage and parsley. Combine the yogurt, sugar, lemon juice, mustard, salt and pepper; pour over cabbage mixture and toss to coat. Cover and refrigerate for 6-8 hours. Just before serving, add grapes, almonds and sesame seeds; mix well. **Yield:** 8-10 servings.

Holiday Cookies

SITTIN' PRETTY PEANUT COOKIES
Gloria Hurl, Galloway, Ohio

For fun cookies that look as good as they taste, try this easy recipe. They have lots of peanut flavor, fluffy frosting middles and holiday-colored peanut M&M's on top.

    1/2 cup butter (no substitutes), softened
    1/4 cup packed brown sugar
      1 egg, *separated*
    1/2 teaspoon vanilla extract
      1 cup all-purpose flour
    1/4 teaspoon salt
      1 cup finely chopped peanuts, toasted
    1/2 cup vanilla frosting
Peanut M&M's

In a mixing bowl, cream butter and brown sugar. Beat in egg yolk and vanilla. Combine flour and salt; gradually add to creamed mixture. Cover and refrigerate for 2 hours. Roll into 1-in. balls. In a small bowl, beat egg white. Dip balls in egg white, then roll in peanuts. Place 2 in. apart on ungreased baking sheets.

 Bake at 350° for 5 minutes. Remove from oven; using the end of a wooden spoon handle, make an indentation in the center of each. Bake 7-9 minutes longer or until firm. Remove to wire racks to cool. Fill centers with vanilla frosting and top with M&M's. **Yield:** about 2 dozen.

MACADAMIA ALMOND DELIGHTS
Ethel Marshall, Salem, Oregon

A few years ago, I decided to liven up my basic chocolate chip cookie recipe by adding macadamia nuts, white chocolate chips and almond paste. Since the scrumptious results got such rave reviews from my 26 grandchildren, we've designated this version a "keeper".

    2/3 cup butter (no substitutes), softened
    2/3 cup shortening
      1 cup sugar
      1 cup packed brown sugar
      2 eggs
      2 teaspoons vanilla extract
      1 cup almond paste
      3 cups plus 3 tablespoons all-purpose flour
      1 teaspoon baking soda
      1 teaspoon salt
1-1/2 cups macadamia nuts, chopped
      1 package (11 ounces) vanilla *or* white chips

In a mixing bowl, cream the butter, shortening and sugars. Add eggs, one at a time, beating well after each addition. Beat in vanilla and almond paste. Combine flour, baking soda and salt; gradually add to the creamed mixture and mix well. Stir in nuts and chips.

 Drop by heaping tablespoonfuls 2 in. apart onto ungreased baking sheets. Bake at 350° for 12-15 minutes or until lightly browned. Remove to wire racks to cool. **Yield:** 4 dozen.

SUGARED DATE BALLS
Sandra Vautrain, Sugar Land, Texas

When I was a youngster, Mom always baked these tender old-fashioned cookies dotted with chewy dates and crunchy walnuts. Much to the delight of my family, I've continued her delicious tradition.

    1/2 cup butter (no substitutes), softened
    1/3 cup confectioners' sugar
      1 tablespoon milk
      1 teaspoon vanilla extract
1-1/4 cups all-purpose flour
    1/4 teaspoon salt
    2/3 cup chopped dates
    1/2 cup chopped nuts
Additional confectioners' sugar

In a mixing bowl, cream butter and sugar. Beat in milk and vanilla. Combine flour and salt; gradually add to creamed mixture. Stir in dates and nuts. Roll into 1-in. balls. Place 2 in. apart on ungreased baking sheets. Bake at 325° for 22-25 minutes or until bottoms are lightly browned. Roll warm cookies in confectioners' sugar; cool on wire racks. **Yield:** about 2-1/2 dozen.

CRISP PECAN ROUNDS
Denise DeJong, Pittsburgh, Pennsylvania

I adapted an old recipe to produce these lightly sweet cookies. They have a wonderful cinnamon and nutmeg flavor that makes them a favorite at our house for the holidays.

1-1/2 cups all-purpose flour
    1/4 cup packed brown sugar
      2 tablespoons sugar
    1/2 teaspoon salt
    1/4 teaspoon ground cinnamon
    1/4 teaspoon ground nutmeg
    2/3 cup cold butter (no substitutes)
      2 tablespoons maple syrup
    1/2 cup chopped pecans
GLAZE:
      1 egg yolk
      1 teaspoon water
TOPPING:
1-1/2 teaspoons sugar
    1/2 teaspoon ground cinnamon

In a bowl, combine the first six ingredients. Cut in butter until mixture resembles coarse crumbs. Stir in syrup. Add pecans. Shape into a 12-in. roll; wrap in plastic wrap. Refrigerate for 4 hours or until firm. Unwrap and cut into 1/4-in. slices. Place 1 in. apart on ungreased baking sheets.

 For glaze, beat egg yolk and water. For topping, combine sugar and cinnamon. Brush glaze over cookies and sprinkle with cinnamon-sugar. Bake at 325° for 20-25 minutes or until golden brown. Remove to wire racks to cool. **Yield:** about 3-1/2 dozen.

SOFT SUGAR COOKIE PUFFS

D. Elaine Rutschke, Spruce View, Alberta
(Pictured at right)

My husband's Aunt Laurel always made these cake-like cookies with her own farm-fresh eggs, cream and butter. Now I prepare batches for Christmas each year. We like them because they're not overly sweet.

        3 eggs
        1 cup whipping cream
        1 cup sugar
        2 teaspoons butter (no substitutes), melted
        1 teaspoon almond extract
        4 cups all-purpose flour
        4 teaspoons baking powder
Assorted colored sugars, optional

In a mixing bowl, beat eggs; add cream and beat well. Beat in the sugar, butter and almond extract. Combine flour and baking powder; gradually add to sugar mixture. Cover and refrigerate for 1 hour or until easy to handle.

On a lightly floured surface, roll out dough to 1/4-in. thickness. Cut with 2-1/2-in. cookie cutters dipped in flour. Place 1 in. apart on greased baking sheets. Sprinkle with colored sugars if desired. Bake at 375° for 10-12 minutes or until edges are lightly browned. Remove to wire racks to cool. **Yield:** about 6 dozen.

PECAN CHOCOLATE PUDDLES

Joyce Kutzler, Clinton, Minnesota

Since my grandchildren like frosted cookies, I came up with this chocolate-topped version that satisfies them and is almost fuss-free for me. I have used the recipe for years and now make them for my great-grandchildren.

    1/2 cup butter (no substitutes), softened
        1 cup packed brown sugar
        1 egg
        1 teaspoon vanilla extract
        1 cup all-purpose flour
    1/2 cup quick-cooking oats
    1/2 teaspoon salt
    1/2 teaspoon baking powder
        1 cup chopped pecans
        1 cup (6 ounces) miniature semisweet chocolate
          chips
FILLING:
        1 cup (6 ounces) semisweet chocolate chips
    1/2 cup sweetened condensed milk
      48 pecan halves

In a mixing bowl, cream butter and brown sugar. Beat in egg and vanilla. Combine the flour, oats, salt and baking powder; gradually add to creamed mixture. Stir in chopped pecans and miniature chocolate chips. In a saucepan, melt chocolate chips with milk; stir until smooth. Roll dough into 1-in. balls. Place 2 in. apart on ungreased baking sheets.

Using the end of a wooden spoon handle, make an indentation in the center of each ball. Fill with a rounded teaspoonful of melted chocolate; top with a pecan half. Bake at 350° for 14-16 minutes or until the edges are lightly browned. Remove to wire racks to cool. **Yield:** 4 dozen.

MERRY CHERRY BARS

Judith Dial, Hampton, Virginia

These luscious bars, filled with cherries and almonds, really suit the Christmas season. I sometimes put a cup of coconut in a clean jar with a few drops of red food coloring. After a few shakes, I have tinted coconut to sprinkle on top.

        2 cups all-purpose flour
    1/2 cup confectioners' sugar
        1 cup cold butter (no substitutes)
FILLING:
1-1/2 cups packed brown sugar
        2 eggs
    1/4 cup all-purpose flour
    1/2 teaspoon baking powder
    1/2 teaspoon salt
        1 cup finely chopped almonds
    1/2 cup finely chopped maraschino cherries,
          drained
CHERRY ICING:
        2 cups confectioners' sugar
    1/4 cup cherry juice
        3 tablespoons butter (no substitutes), softened
    1/2 teaspoon almond extract

In a bowl, combine flour and confectioners' sugar; cut in butter until crumbly. Press into a greased 13-in. x 9-in. x 2-in. baking pan. Bake at 350° for 12-15 minutes or until lightly browned.

Meanwhile, in a mixing bowl, combine brown sugar and eggs; mix well. Combine flour, baking powder and salt; gradually add to egg mixture. Stir in almonds and cherries. Spread over crust. Bake at 350° for 30-35 minutes or until bars begin to pull away from sides of pan. Cool on a wire rack. In a small mixing bowl, beat icing ingredients until smooth. Frost bars. **Yield:** 3 dozen.

CREATIVE COOKIE COLLECTION. Shown clockwise from top right: Crispy Norwegian Bows (p. 35), Peanut Butter Pinwheels (p. 34), Painted Holiday Delights (p. 34), Gingerbread Boys (p. 34) and Peppermint Brownies (p. 34).

PEANUT BUTTER PINWHEELS
Kandy Dick, Junction, Texas
(Pictured on page 33)

These doubly delightful pinwheel cookies are very easy to prepare. They feature the classic combination of peanut butter and chocolate in an attractive swirl.

  1/2 cup shortening
  1/2 cup creamy peanut butter
    1 cup sugar
    1 egg
    2 tablespoons milk
1-1/4 cups all-purpose flour
  1/2 teaspoon baking soda
  1/2 teaspoon salt
    1 cup (6 ounces) semisweet chocolate chips

In a mixing bowl, cream shortening, peanut butter and sugar. Beat in egg and milk. Combine the flour, baking soda and salt; gradually add to creamed mixture. Roll out between waxed paper into a 12-in. x 10-in. rectangle. Melt chocolate chips; cool slightly. Spread over dough to within 1/2 in. of edges. Roll up tightly, jelly-roll style, starting with a long side; wrap in plastic wrap. Refrigerate for 20-30 minutes or until easy to handle.

    Unwrap dough and cut into 1/4-in. slices. Place 1 in. apart on greased baking sheets. Bake at 375° for 10-12 minutes or until edges are lightly browned. Remove to wire racks to cool. **Yield:** about 4 dozen.

PEPPERMINT BROWNIES
Marcy Greenblatt, Redding, California
(Pictured on page 32)

My grandmother encouraged me to enter these mint brownies in the county fair some years ago—and they earned top honors! They're a great chewy treat to serve during the holidays.

  3/4 cup vegetable oil
    2 cups sugar
    2 teaspoons vanilla extract
    4 eggs
1-1/3 cups all-purpose flour
    1 cup baking cocoa
    1 teaspoon baking powder
    1 teaspoon salt
  3/4 cup crushed peppermint candy, *divided*
GLAZE:
    1 cup (6 ounces) semisweet chocolate chips
    1 tablespoon shortening

Line a 13-in. x 9-in. x 2-in. baking pan with foil; grease the foil and set aside. In a mixing bowl, beat oil and sugar. Stir in vanilla. Add eggs, one at a time, beating well after each addition. Combine the flour, cocoa, baking powder and salt; gradually add to creamed mixture. Set aside 2 tablespoons peppermint candy for garnish; stir remaining candy into creamed mixture. Spread into prepared pan.

    Bake at 350° for 35-40 minutes or until a toothpick inserted near the center comes out clean. Cool on a wire rack. For glaze, melt chocolate chips and shortening in a microwave or heavy saucepan; stir until smooth. Spread over brownies; sprinkle with reserved candy. **Yield:** 2 dozen.

GINGERBREAD BOYS
Doré Merrick Grabski, Utica, New York
(Pictured on page 32)

These lightly spiced festive fellows are great to munch on. And if I punch a hole in the cutout shapes before baking, I can use the sturdy cookies as tree ornaments, too.

  2/3 cup shortening
  1/2 cup sugar
  1/2 cup molasses
    1 egg
    3 cups all-purpose flour
    1 teaspoon baking soda
    1 teaspoon *each* ground cinnamon, ginger and
      cloves
  1/2 teaspoon salt
  1/2 teaspoon ground nutmeg
Confectioners' sugar icing, red-hot candies and
    miniature chocolate chips, optional

In a mixing bowl, cream shortening and sugar. Add molasses and egg; mix well. Combine the flour, baking soda, cinnamon, ginger, cloves, salt and nutmeg; gradually add to creamed mixture and mix well. Divide dough in half. Refrigerate for at least 2 hours.

    On a lightly floured surface, roll out each portion of dough to 1/8-in. thickness. Cut with a 4-in. cookie cutter dipped in flour. Place 2 in. apart on greased baking sheets. Bake at 350° for 9-11 minutes or until edges are firm. Remove to wire racks to cool. Decorate as desired. **Yield:** about 2 dozen.

PAINTED HOLIDAY DELIGHTS
Judy Degenstein, Ottawa, Kansas
(Pictured on page 33)

These soft sandwich cookies are eye-catching, thanks to the holiday designs you paint on with food coloring. Orange juice in the dough and strawberry preserves in the filling add a light fruity flavor. I make them for special occasions.

    2 cups all-purpose flour
  1/2 cup sugar
  1/2 cup confectioners' sugar
    2 teaspoons ground cinnamon
  3/4 teaspoon baking powder
  1/4 teaspoon salt
  1/2 cup cold butter (no substitutes)
    1 egg
  1/4 cup orange juice
FILLING:
    1 package (8 ounces) cream cheese, softened
    3 tablespoons confectioners' sugar
    3 tablespoons strawberry preserves
GLAZE:
    1 cup confectioners' sugar
  1/4 teaspoon vanilla extract
    1 to 2 tablespoons milk
Assorted food coloring

In a bowl, combine the first six ingredients. Cut in butter until mixture resembles coarse crumbs. Combine egg and orange juice; stir into crumb mixture just until moistened. Shape into a ball; cover and chill for 1-2 hours or until easy to handle. On a floured surface, roll out dough to 1/8-in. thickness. Cut with a 2-in. round cookie cutter. Place 1 in. apart on ungreased baking sheets. Bake at 375° for 8-10 minutes or until lightly browned. Remove to wire racks to cool.

Combine filling ingredients; spread on the bottom of half of the cookies. Top with remaining cookies. For glaze, combine sugar, vanilla and enough milk to achieve desired consistency. Spread over tops of cookies; dry. Using a small new paintbrush and food coloring, paint holiday designs on cookie tops. Store in the refrigerator. **Yield:** about 2 dozen.

CRISPY NORWEGIAN BOWS
Janie Norwood, Albany, Georgia
(Pictured on page 33)

I've been fixing these cookies for so long, I don't recall where the recipe came from. They're a "must" at our house.

    3 egg yolks
    3 tablespoons sugar
    3 tablespoons whipping cream
1/2 teaspoon ground cardamom
    1 to 1-1/4 cups all-purpose flour
Oil for deep-fat frying
Confectioners' sugar

In a mixing bowl, beat egg yolks and sugar until light and lemon-colored. Add cream and cardamom; mix well. Gradually add flour until dough is firm enough to roll. On a lightly floured surface, roll into a 15-in. square. Using a pastry wheel or knife, cut into 15-in. x 1-1/2-in. strips; cut diagonally at 2-1/2-in. intervals. In the center of each diamond, make a 1-in. slit; pull one end through slit.

In an electric skillet or deep-fat fryer, heat oil to 375°. Fry bows, a few at a time, for 20-40 seconds or until golden brown on both sides. Drain on paper towels. Dust with confectioners' sugar. **Yield:** 4 dozen.

CASHEW TASSIE CUPS
Lois Zimmerman, Plymouth, Nebraska

These little treats are packed with plenty of flavor. The nutty filling sits in rich-tasting mini pastry shells. Delicious!

1/2 cup butter (no substitutes), softened
    1 package (3 ounces) cream cheese, softened
    1 cup all-purpose flour
FILLING:
  2/3 cup coarsely chopped cashews
1/2 cup packed brown sugar
    1 egg
    1 teaspoon vanilla extract

In a mixing bowl, beat butter and cream cheese until smooth; stir in flour. Shape into 1-in. balls. Press dough onto the bottom and up the sides of ungreased miniature muffin cups. Spoon cashews into shells; set aside.

In another mixing bowl, beat the brown sugar, egg and vanilla until combined; spoon over nuts. Bake at 350° for 20-25 minutes or until filling is set and pastry is golden brown. Cool for 1 minute before removing from pans to wire racks. **Yield:** 2 dozen.

WHITE CHOCOLATE PUMPKIN DREAMS
Jean Kleckner, Seattle, Washington

If you like pumpkin pie, you'll love these delicious pumpkin cookies dotted with white chocolate chips and chopped pecans. Drizzled with a brown sugar icing, they're irresistible.

    1 cup butter (no substitutes), softened
1/2 cup sugar
1/2 cup packed brown sugar
    1 egg
    2 teaspoons vanilla extract
    1 cup cooked *or* canned pumpkin
    2 cups all-purpose flour
3-1/2 teaspoons pumpkin pie spice
    1 teaspoon baking powder
    1 teaspoon baking soda
1/4 teaspoon salt
    1 package (11 ounces) vanilla *or* white chips
    1 cup chopped pecans
PENUCHE FROSTING:
  1/2 cup packed brown sugar
    3 tablespoons butter (no substitutes)
  1/4 cup milk
1-1/2 to 2 cups confectioners' sugar

In a mixing bowl, cream butter and sugars. Beat in egg, vanilla and pumpkin. Combine dry ingredients; gradually add to the creamed mixture. Stir in chips and pecans. Drop by rounded teaspoonfuls 2 in. apart onto ungreased baking sheets. Bake at 350° for 12-14 minutes or until firm. Remove to wire racks to cool.

For frosting, combine brown sugar and butter in a saucepan. Bring to a boil; cook over medium heat for 1 minute or until slightly thickened. Cool for 10 minutes. Add milk; beat until smooth. Beat in enough confectioners' sugar to reach desired consistency. Frost cookies. **Yield:** about 4-1/2 dozen.

ALMOND CHOCOLATE COOKIES
Sharon Knipe, Fort Madison, Iowa

With crisp outsides and brownie-like insides, these cookies were a big hit when my 5-year-old son took a batch to share at preschool. In fact, kids of all ages love them.

    1 cup butter (no substitutes), softened
3/4 cup packed brown sugar
2/3 cup sugar
1/2 cup baking cocoa
    2 to 3 teaspoons almond extract
    1 teaspoon vanilla extract
    2 eggs
2-1/4 cups all-purpose flour
    1 teaspoon baking soda

In a mixing bowl, beat the butter, sugars, cocoa and extracts until creamy. Add eggs, one at a time, beating well after each addition. Combine the flour and baking soda; gradually add to sugar mixture. Drop by rounded teaspoonfuls 2 in. apart onto ungreased baking sheets. Bake at 375° for 7-9 minutes or until edges are firm. Remove to wire racks to cool. **Yield:** about 6-1/2 dozen.

TASTY TREATS. Shown from top to bottom: Peppermint Hard Candy (p. 37), Layered Mint Candies (p. 37) and Snowballs (p. 37).

Seasonal Sweets

LAYERED MINT CANDIES
Rhonda Vauble, Sac City, Iowa
(Pictured on page 36)

These incredible melt-in-your-mouth candies have the perfect amount of mint nestled between layers of mild chocolate. Even when I make a double batch for everyone to enjoy, the supply never lasts long at Christmas!

    1 tablespoon butter (no substitutes)
1-1/2 pounds white candy coating, *divided*
    1 cup (6 ounces) semisweet chocolate chips
    1 teaspoon peppermint extract
    4 drops green food coloring, optional
    3 tablespoons whipping cream

Line a 13-in. x 9-in. x 2-in. baking pan with foil. Grease the foil with 1 tablespoon butter; set aside. In a microwave or heavy saucepan, melt 1 pound candy coating and chocolate chips. Spread half into prepared pan; set remaining mixture aside. Melt remaining candy coating; stir in extract and food coloring if desired. Stir in cream until smooth (mixture will be stiff). Spread over first layer; refrigerate for 10 minutes or until firm.

Warm reserved chocolate mixture if necessary; spread over mint layer. Refrigerate for 1 hour or until firm. Lift out of the pan with foil and remove the foil. Cut into 1-in. squares. Store in an airtight container in the refrigerator. **Yield:** about 2 pounds (about 9-1/2 dozen).

SNOWBALLS
Muriel White, Brampton, Ontario
(Pictured on page 36)

I've been making these popular treats for 40 years, much to my family's delight. They look impressive with chocolate and coconut wrapped around a chewy marshmallow center, yet they're surprisingly simple to assemble.

    1/2 cup butter (no substitutes)
    1 can (14 ounces) sweetened condensed milk
    3 tablespoons baking cocoa
    1 teaspoon vanilla extract
    2 cups graham cracker crumbs (about 32 squares)
3-1/2 cups flaked coconut, *divided*
    32 to 36 large marshmallows

Line a baking sheet with waxed paper; set aside. In a saucepan, combine the butter, milk, cocoa and vanilla. Cook and stir over medium heat until butter is melted and mixture is smooth. Remove from the heat; stir in cracker crumbs and 1-1/2 cups coconut. Let stand until cool enough to handle.

Using moistened hands, wrap about 1 tablespoon of mixture around each marshmallow (dip hands in water often to prevent sticking). Roll in remaining coconut; place on prepared baking sheet. Cover and freeze until firm. Store in an airtight container in the refrigerator or freezer. May be frozen for up to 2 months. **Yield:** about 3 dozen.

PEPPERMINT HARD CANDY
Lois Ostenson, Aneta, North Dakota
(Pictured on page 36)

This easy-to-make clear hard candy has a mint flavor from the combination of peppermint and vanilla extracts. Plus, the eye-catching sweets won't stick to your teeth.

    1 tablespoon butter (no substitutes)
    2 cups sugar
    1 cup light corn syrup
    1 to 1-1/2 teaspoons peppermint extract
    1 teaspoon vanilla extract
    6 to 8 drops green food coloring, optional

Line a 13-in. x 9-in. x 2-in. baking pan with foil. Grease the foil with 1 tablespoon butter; set aside. In a large heavy saucepan, combine sugar and corn syrup. Bring to a boil over medium heat, stirring occasionally. Cover and cook for 3 minutes to dissolve sugar crystals. Uncover; cook over medium-high heat, without stirring, until a candy thermometer reads 300° (hard-crack stage).

Remove from the heat; stir in extracts and food coloring. Pour into prepared pan. Cool; break into pieces. Store in airtight containers. **Yield:** about 1-1/4 pounds.

Editor's Note: See the box on page 39 for information about testing your candy thermometer.

NUT 'N' CORN CLUSTERS
Maryeileen Jahnke, South Milwaukee, Wisconsin

I can tell this recipe has served me faithfully for a long time by the old dog-eared recipe card. These crisp caramel corn clusters are a holiday treat my family enjoys munching.

    5 quarts popped popcorn
    2 cups mixed nuts
1-1/2 teaspoons butter (no substitutes)
    1 cup sugar
    1/2 cup honey
    1/2 cup corn syrup
    1 cup peanut butter
    1 teaspoon vanilla extract
    1 teaspoon molasses

Line baking sheets with waxed paper; set aside. Combine popcorn and nuts in a large roasting pan; place in a 250° oven. Meanwhile, grease the sides of a heavy saucepan with 1-1/2 teaspoons butter. Combine the sugar, honey and corn syrup in saucepan. Bring to a boil over medium heat, stirring constantly. Boil for 2 minutes without stirring.

Remove from the heat; stir in peanut butter, vanilla and molasses. Pour over warm popcorn mixture and stir to coat. Working quickly, use buttered hands to form mixture into 1-1/2-in. clusters. Place on prepared baking sheets to dry. Store in an airtight container at room temperature. **Yield:** about 12 dozen.

Editor's Note: If mixture becomes too firm to form into clusters, rewarm in a 250° oven for a few minutes.

TOFFEE CHIP FUDGE
Maxine Smith, Owanka, South Dakota

My grandchildren savor the job of taste-testing my baking experiments. I combined two recipes to come up with this yummy fudge dotted with crisp toffee bits. The kids gave it a "thumbs-up" before requesting a batch to take home.

1-1/2 teaspoons plus 1/4 cup butter (no substitutes), *divided*
1-1/2 cups sugar
   1 can (5 ounces) evaporated milk
  1/4 teaspoon salt
   2 cups (12 ounces) semisweet chocolate chips
   2 cups miniature marshmallows
  1/2 cup plus 2 tablespoons English toffee bits or almond brickle chips, *divided*
   1 teaspoon vanilla extract

Line a 9-in. square baking pan with foil. Grease the foil with 1-1/2 teaspoons butter; set aside. In a large heavy saucepan, combine the sugar, milk, salt and remaining butter. Cook and stir over medium heat until sugar is dissolved. Bring to a rapid boil; boil for 5 minutes, stirring constantly.

Remove from the heat; stir in chocolate chips and marshmallows until melted. Fold in 1/2 cup toffee bits and vanilla; mix well. Pour into prepared pan. Sprinkle with remaining toffee bits. Chill until firm. Remove from pan and cut into 1-in. squares. Store in the refrigerator. **Yield:** 2 pounds.

COCONUT CASHEW BRITTLE
Darlene Markel, Mt. Hood, Oregon

This rich buttery brittle has always been part of our Christmas candy collection. Lots of coconut and cashews ensures it's extra scrumptious.

   2 cups cashew halves
   2 cups flaked coconut
   2 cups sugar
   1 cup light corn syrup
  1/2 cup plus 1 teaspoon water, *divided*
   1 cup butter (no substitutes), cubed
   2 teaspoons vanilla extract
1-1/2 teaspoons baking soda

Combine cashews and coconut on a 15-in. x 10-in. x 1-in. baking pan. Bake at 350° for 8-10 minutes or until golden brown, stirring occasionally. Butter two baking sheets and warm in a 200° oven.

In a large heavy saucepan, combine sugar, corn syrup and 1/2 cup water. Cook and stir over medium heat until mixture comes to a boil. Add butter; cook and stir until butter is melted. Continue cooking, without stirring, until a candy thermometer reads 300° (hard-crack stage).

Meanwhile, combine the vanilla, baking soda and remaining water. Remove saucepan from the heat; add cashews and coconut. Stir in baking soda mixture. Quickly pour onto prepared baking sheets. Spread with a buttered metal spatula to 1/4-in. thickness. Cool before breaking into pieces. Store in an airtight container. **Yield:** about 3 pounds.

Editor's Note: See the box on page 39 for information about testing your candy thermometer.

WHITE CHOCOLATE PEANUT BUTTER SQUARES
Gloria Jarrett, Loveland, Ohio

People regularly request the recipe once they try my peanut butter fudge dipped in melted white chocolate. It's a nice contrast to typical chocolates on a candy platter.

   1 tablespoon plus 3/4 cup butter (no substitutes)
   3 cups sugar
  2/3 cup evaporated milk
   1 package (10 ounces) peanut butter chips
   1 jar (7 ounces) marshmallow creme
   1 cup chopped nuts
   1 tablespoon vanilla extract
1-1/2 pounds white candy coating
  1/2 cup semisweet chocolate chips, optional
   1 teaspoon shortening, optional

Line a 13-in. x 9-in. x 2-in. baking pan with foil. Grease the foil with 1 tablespoon butter; set aside. In a heavy saucepan, combine the sugar, evaporated milk and remaining butter. Bring to a boil over medium heat; boil for 5 minutes, stirring constantly. Remove from the heat; stir in the peanut butter chips until melted. Add the marshmallow creme, nuts and vanilla; stir until blended. Pour into prepared pan. Cool.

Remove from pan and cut into 1-in. squares. Place on waxed paper-lined baking sheets; freeze or refrigerate until firm. In a microwave or heavy saucepan, melt the candy coating, stirring often. Dip the squares in coating; place on waxed paper-lined baking sheets until set. If desired, melt the chocolate chips and shortening; drizzle over the squares. Store in an airtight container. **Yield:** 3-1/4 pounds (about 9-1/2 dozen).

LICORICE CARAMEL CANDY
Paula Fischer, Rapid City, South Dakota

These delicious treats are a fun cross between caramels and licorice. I always get compliments on them—especially from those who enjoy black licorice.

1-1/2 teaspoons butter (no substitutes)
   2 cups sugar
   3 cups whipping cream, *divided*
1-1/3 cups light corn syrup
   2 teaspoons anise extract
  1/4 to 1/2 teaspoon red or black paste food coloring

Line an 8-in. square pan with foil. Grease the foil with 1-1/2 teaspoons butter; set aside. In a heavy Dutch oven, combine the sugar, 1-1/2 cups cream and corn syrup. Bring to a boil over medium heat, stirring constantly. Cook and stir until a candy thermometer reads 234° (soft-ball stage). Gradually add remaining cream; return to a boil, stirring constantly, until a candy thermometer reads 248° (firm-ball stage).

Remove from the heat; stir in extract and food coloring if desired (keep face away from mixture as odor is very strong). Pour into prepared pan (do not scrape pan). Cool completely before cutting. Store in an airtight container in the refrigerator. **Yield:** about 1 pound (about 4 dozen).

Editor's Note: See the box on page 39 for information about testing your candy thermometer.

GLAZED ALMONDS
Katie Koziolek, Hartland, Minnesota

These glossy candy-coated almonds are almost like brittle but much easier to make. With the sweet and salty combination, it's hard to stop munching these delicious nuts.

    4 tablespoons butter (no substitutes), *divided*
    2 cups blanched whole almonds
    3/4 cup sugar
    1 teaspoon vanilla extract
    1/2 teaspoon salt

Line a baking sheet with foil. Grease the foil with 1 tablespoon butter; set aside. In a large heavy skillet, combine the almonds, sugar and remaining butter. Cook and stir over medium heat for 6-8 minutes or until sugar is golden brown.

Remove from the heat; carefully stir in vanilla. Spread onto prepared baking sheet; immediately sprinkle with salt. Cool before breaking into pieces. Store in an airtight container. **Yield:** about 1 pound.

HOLIDAY SNACK MIX
Rosanne Weigley, Tempe, Arizona

I'm not much of a cook, but my friend insisted that even I could make this awesome mix. She was right! People rave over it whenever I give it as a gift or share it at a gathering.

    5 cups Rice Chex
    4 cups Corn Chex
    3 cups Golden Grahams
    1 cup flaked coconut
    1 cup slivered almonds
    3/4 cup butter or margarine
    1 cup sugar
    1 cup light corn syrup

Grease two 15-in. x 10-in. x 1-in. baking pans; set aside. In a large bowl, combine cereals, coconut and almonds; set aside. In a heavy saucepan, combine the butter, sugar and corn syrup. Bring to a boil over medium heat, stirring constantly. Boil for 10 minutes, stirring occasionally. Pour over cereal mixture and stir until well coated. Spread onto prepared pans. Cool, stirring occasionally. Store in airtight containers. **Yield:** 3-1/2 quarts.

COCONUT PEAKS
Patricia Shinn, Fruitland Park, Florida

I found this gem on a slip of paper in a cookbook I got at a yard sale. The candies get great flavor from browned butter. I've received many requests for this recipe over the years.

    1/4 cup butter (no substitutes)
    3 cups flaked coconut
    2 cups confectioners' sugar
    1/4 cup half-and-half cream
    1 cup (6 ounces) semisweet chocolate chips
    2 teaspoons shortening

Line a baking sheet with waxed paper; set aside. In a

saucepan, cook butter over medium-low heat until golden brown, about 5 minutes. Remove from the heat; stir in the coconut, sugar and cream. Drop by rounded teaspoonfuls onto prepared baking sheet. Refrigerate until easy to handle, about 25 minutes.

Roll mixture into balls, then shape each into a cone. Return to baking sheet; refrigerate for 15 minutes. In a microwave or heavy saucepan, melt chocolate chips and shortening. Dip bottoms of cones into chocolate. Return to waxed paper to harden. Store in an airtight container in the refrigerator. **Yield:** about 3 dozen.

BUTTERSCOTCH COCONUT SQUARES
Eve Campbell, Crysler, Ontario

My former boss used to prepare these sweet morsels for her staff at Christmas. When I got the recipe, I was thrilled to discover they're not hard to make.

    1-1/2 teaspoons plus 1/2 cup butter (no substitutes),
        divided
    1 package (11 ounces) butterscotch chips
    1 cup peanut butter
    1 cup miniature marshmallows
    1/2 cup flaked coconut

Grease a 9-in. square pan with 1-1/2 teaspoons butter; set aside. In a microwave or heavy saucepan, melt the butterscotch chips, peanut butter and remaining butter until smooth. Cool for 20 minutes. Stir in marshmallows just until combined (do not melt marshmallows). Pour into prepared pan; sprinkle with coconut. Refrigerate, uncovered, for 2 hours or until firm. Cut into 1-in. pieces. Store in an airtight container. **Yield:** about 6-1/2 dozen.

MINT CHOCOLATE COOKIE CRUNCH
Kathy Kelzer, St. Louis Park, Minnesota

I usually give a different homemade treat to my nieces and nephews every Christmas. This rich no-bake candy was a hit. With just four ingredients, it's easy enough for kids to make.

    3 packages (12 ounces each) semisweet
        chocolate chips
    1 to 1-1/2 teaspoons peppermint extract
    1 package (20 ounces) chocolate cream-filled
        sandwich cookies, coarsely crushed
    4 cups crisp rice cereal

Line baking sheets with waxed paper; set aside. In a microwave or heavy saucepan, melt chocolate chips. Stir in extract. Combine cookies and cereal in a large bowl. Add chocolate mixture and stir to coat. Drop by tablespoonfuls onto prepared baking sheets; cool. Store in airtight containers at room temperature. **Yield:** about 8 dozen.

● We recommend that you test your candy thermometer before each use by bringing water to a boil; the thermometer should read 212°. Adjust your recipe temperature up or down based on your test.

DELICIOUS HOLIDAY DESSERTS.
Shown clockwise from top left: Strawberry Angel Trifle (p. 41), Linzertorte (p. 41) and Chocolate Yule Log (p. 41).

Festive Desserts

STRAWBERRY ANGEL TRIFLE
Lucille Belsham, Fort Fraser, British Columbia
(Pictured on page 40)

I always get compliments when I bring this attractive and tasty trifle out of the refrigerator. Not only does it serve a big group nicely, I can make it ahead of time, too.

> 1 package (16 ounces) one-step angel food
>   cake mix
> 1 package (6 ounces) strawberry gelatin
> 3/4 cup plus 1/3 cup sugar, *divided*
> 2 cups boiling water
> 5 cups fresh *or* frozen unsweetened strawberries,
>   thawed and drained
> 2 cups whipping cream

Prepare and bake cake mix according to package directions; cool completely. In a large bowl, dissolve gelatin and 3/4 cup sugar in boiling water. Mash half of the strawberries; add to gelatin mixture. Refrigerate until slightly thickened, about 1 hour. Slice remaining strawberries; stir into the gelatin.

Cut cake into 1-in. cubes. Place half in a 3-qt. trifle or glass bowl. Top with half of the gelatin mixture. Repeat. Cover and refrigerate until set, about 4 hours. In a mixing bowl, beat cream until soft peaks form. Gradually add remaining sugar, beating until stiff peaks form. Spoon over gelatin. **Yield:** 12-16 servings.

LINZERTORTE
Jeanne Siebert, Salt Lake City, Utah
(Pictured on page 40)

My Austrian grandmother made this nutty jam-filled dessert only at Christmastime. So did my mother, and now I'm proud to carry on the tasty tradition. It's a great way to end a holiday meal.

> 2 cups all-purpose flour
> 2 cups ground hazelnuts *or* walnuts
> 1/2 cup sugar
> 1/2 cup packed brown sugar
> 1 teaspoon ground cinnamon
> 1/8 teaspoon salt
> Dash ground cloves
> 1 cup cold butter (no substitutes)
> 2 eggs, lightly beaten
> 1 teaspoon grated lemon peel
> 1-1/3 cups raspberry jam
> Confectioners' sugar, optional

In a bowl, combine the first seven ingredients. Cut in butter until mixture resembles coarse crumbs. Add eggs and lemon peel; stir until mixture forms a ball. Divide into fourths. Cover and refrigerate for 3-4 hours or until chilled. Remove two portions of dough from refrigerator; press each into an ungreased 9-in. fluted tart pan with removable bottom. Spread 2/3 cup jam over each.

Between two sheets of lightly floured waxed paper, roll one portion of remaining dough into a 10-in. x 6-in. rectangle. Cut six 1-in.-wide strips; arrange in a lattice design over jam. Repeat with remaining dough (return dough to the refrigerator if needed). Bake at 350° for 40-45 minutes or until bubbly and crust is browned. Cool completely. Dust with confectioners' sugar if desired. **Yield:** 2 tortes (8 servings each).

CHOCOLATE YULE LOG
Bernadette Colvin, Houston, Texas
(Pictured on page 40)

For many years, this impressive rolled cake has been a favorite Christmas dessert for our family—everyone just loves it! Plus, I'm always asked to bring the rich chocolaty treat to our annual church Christmas function.

> 4 eggs, *separated*
> 2/3 cup sugar, *divided*
> 1/2 cup all-purpose flour
> 2 tablespoons baking cocoa
> 1 teaspoon baking powder
> 1/4 teaspoon salt
> **FILLING:**
> 1 cup whipping cream
> 2 tablespoons sugar
> 1/4 teaspoon almond extract
> **FROSTING:**
> 1/2 cup butter (no substitutes), softened
> 2 cups confectioners' sugar
> 2 squares (1 ounce *each*) unsweetened chocolate,
>   melted
> 2 tablespoons milk
> 2 teaspoons vanilla extract

Line a greased 15-in. x 10-in. x 1-in. baking pan with waxed paper; grease the paper and set aside. In a mixing bowl, beat egg yolks until light and fluffy. Gradually add 1/3 cup sugar, beating until light and lemon-colored, about 5 minutes. In another mixing bowl, beat egg whites until foamy. Gradually add remaining sugar, beating until stiff peaks form. Fold into egg yolks, a third at a time. Combine the flour, cocoa, baking powder and salt; fold into egg mixture, a third at a time.

Spread batter into prepared pan. Bake at 375° for 10-12 minutes or until cake springs back when lightly touched. Cool for 5 minutes. Turn cake onto a kitchen towel dusted with confectioners' sugar. Gently peel off waxed paper. Roll up cake in the towel, jelly-roll style, starting with a short side; cool completely on a wire rack.

Meanwhile, for the filling, beat the cream in a mixing bowl until soft peaks form. Gradually add the sugar and the almond extract, beating until almost stiff. Unroll the cake; spread the filling to within 1 in. of edges. Reroll cake. In a mixing bowl, cream the butter and confectioners' sugar. Beat in the chocolate, milk and vanilla until smooth. Frost the cake, using a metal spatula to create a bark-like effect. **Yield:** 14-16 servings.

CRANBERRY-APPLE MINCEMEAT PIES
Lucinda Burton, Scarborough, Ontario

Traditional mincemeat is too heavy for me, but this fruity version hits the spot. Others agree—few folks who've tried it stop at just one slice!

          4 cups fresh *or* frozen cranberries, thawed
          4 cups chopped peeled tart apples
    1-1/2 cups chopped dried apricots
    1-1/2 cups golden raisins
          1 medium unpeeled navel orange, finely chopped
      1/4 cup *each* red and green candied cherries
    2-3/4 cups sugar
          1 cup apple juice
      1/4 cup butter *or* margarine
      1/4 cup orange marmalade
          1 teaspoon ground ginger
      3/4 teaspoon *each* ground allspice, cinnamon and
             nutmeg
    Pastry for double-crust pie (9 inches)

In a Dutch oven or large kettle, combine the fruit, sugar, apple juice, butter, marmalade and spices. Bring to a boil over medium heat. Reduce heat; simmer, uncovered, for 50-60 minutes, stirring occasionally. Cool completely or refrigerate for up to 1 week.

Line two 9-in. pie plates with pastry; trim and flute edges. Divide filling between crusts. Cover edges loosely with foil. Bake at 400° for 20 minutes. Remove foil. Bake 20-25 minutes longer or until crust is golden brown and filling is bubbly. Cool on wire racks. **Yield:** 2 pies (6-8 servings each).

Editor's Note: Mincemeat mixture may be frozen for up to 3 months. Thaw in the refrigerator.

CHOCOLATE MINT CREAM PIE
Donna Christopher, Crestwood, Missouri

This light, refreshing pie is an ideal way to give your holiday guests a treat without going to a lot of fuss. What's more, it cuts nicely, making it a cinch to serve.

          2 cups crushed chocolate-covered mint cookies
          3 to 4 tablespoons hot water
          1 graham cracker crust (8 inches)
          1 package (3 ounces) cream cheese, softened
      1/3 cup sugar
          2 tablespoons milk
      1/4 teaspoon peppermint extract
          1 carton (8 ounces) frozen whipped topping, thawed
          6 to 10 drops green food coloring, optional

Set aside 2 tablespoons cookie crumbs for garnish. In a bowl, combine remaining crumbs with enough hot water to make crumbs spreadable. Spoon over the graham cracker crust; spread out evenly; set aside. In a mixing bowl, beat cream cheese until fluffy. Add the sugar, milk and extract; beat until smooth. Fold in whipped topping.

If food coloring is desired, divide mixture in half and add coloring to one half. Alternately spoon mounds of plain and colored mixture into crust; swirl with a knife. Sprinkle with reserved cookie crumbs. Cover and refrigerate for 3 hours or until firm. **Yield:** 8-10 servings.

SALTED PEANUT CAKE
Kay Beauchamp, Marquette, Michigan

My mother-in-law shared this treasured family recipe with me. We adore the tender nutty cake with its smooth frosting. When my husband, Ralph, finds I've fixed this dessert, he's one happy man!

      1/2 cup shortening
          1 cup sugar
          1 egg
    1-1/2 cups all-purpose flour
          1 teaspoon baking soda
          1 teaspoon baking powder
          1 cup buttermilk
          1 pound salted peanuts, ground
    FROSTING:
      1/2 cup all-purpose flour
          1 cup milk
          1 cup butter *or* margarine, softened
          1 cup confectioners' sugar
          1 teaspoon vanilla extract

In a mixing bowl, cream shortening and sugar. Add egg; beat well. Combine the flour, baking soda and baking powder; add to creamed mixture alternately with buttermilk. Set aside 3/4 cup peanuts for topping. Stir remaining peanuts into batter. Spread into a greased 13-in. x 9-in. x 2-in. baking pan. Bake at 350° for 40-45 minutes or until a toothpick inserted near the center comes out clean. Cool on a wire rack.

Meanwhile, for the frosting, combine the flour and the milk in a saucepan until smooth. Bring to a boil over medium heat, stirring frequently. Cook and stir for 2 minutes or until thickened. Remove from the heat; cool completely. In a mixing bowl, cream the butter and the confectioners' sugar until fluffy. Add the cooled flour mixture and the vanilla; beat until fluffy, about 4 minutes. Spread over the cake; sprinkle with the reserved peanuts. **Yield:** 16-20 servings.

CRANBERRY-TOPPED CAKE
Helen Vail, Glenside, Pennsylvania

For me, part of the joy of Christmas is sharing tempting treats such as this special cake. I love trying new recipes, but I also rely on classics like this one.

    1-1/3 cups sugar, *divided*
          4 cups fresh *or* frozen cranberries, thawed
    CAKE:
          2 cups all-purpose flour
    1-1/2 cups sugar
          1 tablespoon baking powder
          1 teaspoon salt
          5 egg yolks
      3/4 cup cold water
      1/2 cup vegetable oil
    2-1/2 teaspoons vanilla extract
    2-1/2 teaspoons grated lemon peel
          7 egg whites
      1/2 teaspoon cream of tartar
    FROSTING:
          2 cups whipping cream

2 tablespoons sugar
2 teaspoons vanilla extract

Grease the bottoms of two 8-in. square baking dishes; sprinkle each with 1 tablespoon sugar. Sprinkle 2 cups of cranberries over the bottom of each pan; sprinkle with remaining sugar. Cover and bake at 325° for 30 minutes. Uncover; cool for 1 hour.

For cake, combine the flour, sugar, baking powder and salt in a large mixing bowl. Add egg yolks, water, oil, vanilla and lemon peel; beat until smooth, about 1 minute. In another mixing bowl, beat egg whites until foamy. Add cream of tartar; beat until stiff peaks form. Fold a fourth of the egg whites into batter. Fold in remaining whites. Spoon batter over cranberries.

Bake at 325° for 45-55 minutes or until cake springs back when lightly touched. Cool in pans 10 minutes before inverting on wire racks to cool completely. For frosting, beat cream until soft peaks form. Add the sugar and vanilla; beat until stiff peaks form. Spread between layers and over top and sides of cake. Cover and store in the refrigerator. **Yield:** 10-12 servings.

FUDGE MOCHA TORTE
Mary Pajak, Avon Lake, Ohio

This scrumptious elegant cake is not tricky to prepare since it starts with a boxed mix. With its sweet syrup and fluffy chocolate frosting, it's very rich, so you can cut small slices and still satisfy a crowd.

    1 package (18-1/4 ounces) devil's food cake mix
    1 cup (8 ounces) sour cream
    3/4 cup cold strong brewed coffee
    1/3 cup vegetable oil
    3 eggs
    1 teaspoon almond extract
    1/3 cup miniature chocolate chips
SYRUP:
    3 tablespoons warm strong brewed coffee
    3 tablespoons sugar
FROSTING:
    1 cup butter *or* margarine, softened
    1 cup shortening
    2 pounds confectioners' sugar (about 7-1/2 cups)
    2 tablespoons baking cocoa
    3 to 4 tablespoons strong brewed coffee

Line a greased 15-in. x 10-in. x 1-in. baking pan with waxed paper and grease the paper; set aside. In a large mixing bowl, combine cake mix, sour cream, coffee, oil, eggs and extract. Beat on low speed for 30 seconds; beat on medium for 2 minutes. Stir in chips. Pour into prepared pan. Bake at 350° for 22-27 minutes or until a toothpick inserted near the center comes out clean. Cool for 5 minutes before removing from pan to a wire rack. Gently peel off waxed paper.

For the syrup, combine the coffee and sugar; brush over the warm cake. Cool completely. Cut cake into three 10-in. x 5-in. portions. For frosting, cream the butter and the shortening in a mixing bowl until fluffy. Beat in the confectioners' sugar and cocoa. Add the coffee; beat until light and fluffy. Spread 3/4 cup between each layer. Spread remaining frosting over top and sides of cake. **Yield:** 16-18 servings.

MINIATURE ALMOND TARTS
Karen Van Den Berge, Holland, Michigan

My family requests these adorable little tarts each Christmas. I always enjoy making them since the almond paste in the filling reflects our Dutch heritage, plus they're popular at special gatherings.

    1 cup butter *or* margarine, softened
    2 packages (3 ounces *each*) cream cheese, softened
    2 cups all-purpose flour
FILLING:
    6 ounces almond paste, crumbled
    2 eggs, beaten
    1/2 cup sugar
FROSTING:
1-1/2 cups confectioners' sugar
    3 tablespoons butter *or* margarine, softened
    4 to 5 teaspoons milk
Maraschino cherry halves (about 48)

In a mixing bowl, cream the butter and cream cheese. Add flour; mix well. Refrigerate for 1 hour. Shape into 1-in. balls. Place in ungreased miniature muffin cups; press into the bottom and up the sides to form a shell. For filling, combine almond paste, eggs and sugar in a mixing bowl. Beat on low speed until blended. Fill each shell with about 1-1/2 teaspoons filling.

Bake at 325° for 25-30 minutes or until edges are golden brown. Cool for 10 minutes before removing to wire racks to cool completely. For frosting, combine the confectioners' sugar, butter and enough milk to achieve desired consistency. Pipe or spread over tarts. Top each with a cherry half. **Yield:** about 4 dozen.

DATE PUDDING
Sue Eberly, Fayetteville, Pennsylvania

My mother-in-law always whipped up this old-fashioned dessert at Thanksgiving and Christmas. My husband and I enjoy the chewy dates and sweet thick syrup drizzled on top. It's impossible to resist a second helping!

1-1/2 cups packed brown sugar, *divided*
    1 cup water
    1 tablespoon butter *or* margarine
    1 cup all-purpose flour
    2 teaspoons baking powder
    1/4 teaspoon salt
    1/2 cup milk
    1 cup chopped dates
    1/2 cup chopped walnuts
Whipped cream

In a saucepan, bring 1 cup brown sugar and water to a boil. Cook and stir for 3 minutes. Remove from the heat and add butter; set aside. In a bowl, combine the flour, baking powder, salt and remaining brown sugar. Stir in milk until smooth. Add dates and walnuts.

Pour hot brown sugar syrup into an 8-in. square baking dish. Spoon batter over syrup. Bake at 350° for 40-45 minutes or until a toothpick inserted near the center of cake topping comes out clean. Serve warm with whipped cream. **Yield:** 9-12 servings.

GIFTS OF GOODIES. Shown from top to bottom: 3 'C' Bread (p. 45), White Pecan Fudge (p. 45) and Cranberry Butter (p. 45).

3 'C' BREAD
Edna Robinson Bowland, Lakewood, Colorado
(Pictured on page 44)

This sweet bread features carrots, coconut and cherries. That tasty combination ensures each loaf is a welcome gift!

2-1/2 cups all-purpose flour
    1 cup sugar
    1 teaspoon baking powder
    1 teaspoon baking soda
    1 teaspoon ground cinnamon
    1/2 teaspoon salt
    3 eggs
    1/2 cup milk
    1/2 cup vegetable oil
    2 cups shredded carrots
1-1/2 cups flaked coconut
    1/2 cup candied cherries, quartered
    1/2 cup raisins
    1/2 cup chopped pecans

In a large bowl, combine the first six ingredients. In a small bowl, combine the eggs, milk and oil. Stir into dry ingredients just until moistened. Fold in the carrots, coconut, cherries, raisins and pecans. Pour into four greased 5-3/4-in. x 3-in. x 2-in. loaf pans.

Bake at 350° for 40-50 minutes or until a toothpick inserted near the center comes out clean. Cool for 10 minutes before removing from pans to wire racks. Cover and store in the refrigerator. **Yield:** 4 mini loaves.

WHITE PECAN FUDGE
Marie Draper, Price, Utah
(Pictured on page 44)

Each Christmas, I package batches of this rich fudge to send to family and friends. It's just delicious!

    1 tablespoon plus 1/2 cup butter (no substitutes), *divided*
2-1/2 cups miniature marshmallows
2-1/4 cups sugar
    1 cup whipping cream
  16 squares (1 ounce *each*) white baking chocolate, cut into small pieces
    2 teaspoons vanilla extract
    2 cups chopped pecans

Line a 9-in. square pan with foil. Grease the foil with 1/2 tablespoon butter and set aside. Butter the sides of a large heavy saucepan with 1/2 tablespoon butter. Cut remaining butter into small pieces and place in a large heat-proof bowl; add marshmallows and set aside.

In the buttered saucepan, combine sugar and cream. Cook and stir over medium heat until mixture comes to a boil. Cover and cook for 2 minutes to dissolve any sugar crystals. Uncover; cook over medium heat, without stirring, until a candy thermometer reads 234° (soft-ball stage).

Remove from the heat. Pour ove[r] mallows; stir until melted. Add the cho[colate] ring until chocolate is melted and mixture is smooth. Stir in vanilla and nuts. Pour into prepared pan. Refrigerate until firm. Lift out of pan; remove foil and cut into 1-in. squares. Store in an airtight container at room temperature. **Yield:** about 3-1/2 pounds (about 6-1/2 dozen).

Editor's Note: See the box on page 47 for information about testing your candy thermometer.

CRANBERRY BUTTER
Carol Studebaker, Gladstone, Missouri
(Pictured on page 44)

One of my favorite toppings for toast is this tart spread. It's also great spooned over poultry…and ice cream! I've given jars as gifts and have always gotten positive comments.

  10 cups fresh or frozen cranberries
  2/3 cup apple juice
  1/2 to 3/4 cup sugar
    1 cup maple syrup
  1/2 cup honey
  1/2 teaspoon ground cinnamon

In a saucepan over medium heat, bring cranberries, apple juice and sugar to a boil. Cook for 10-15 minutes or until all berries have popped, stirring occasionally. Remove from the heat; cool slightly. Process in batches in a blender or food processor until smooth.

Return cranberry mixture to the saucepan; add remaining ingredients. Bring to a boil over medium heat. Reduce heat; simmer, uncovered, for 10 minutes or until thickened, stirring occasionally. Cover and chill for 8 hours or overnight. Store in the refrigerator. **Yield:** 5 cups.

ZIPPY DRY RUB
Gaynelle Fritsch, Welches, Oregon

Bottles of this spicy blend are fun to share with family and friends. It's a mixture with broad appeal since the rub can be used on all meats or added to rice while it's cooking for a boost of flavor.

    1 tablespoon salt
    1 teaspoon mustard seed
    1 teaspoon pepper
    1 teaspoon chili powder
    1 teaspoon paprika
  1/2 teaspoon ground cumin
  1/2 teaspoon dried coriander
  1/4 teaspoon garlic powder

In a small bowl, combine all ingredients. Store in an airtight container. Rub desired amount onto the surface of uncooked meat. Cover and refrigerate for at least 4 hours before grilling. **Yield:** about 2-1/2 tablespoons.

CARDAMOM TEA BREAD
Sarah Bedia, Lake Jackson, Texas

A cross between pound cake and fruitcake, this bread is especially nice for folks who dislike the heaviness of regular fruitcake. My family enjoys thick slices for breakfast on Christmas morning.

  1/2 cup finely chopped mixed candied fruit
    2 cups all-purpose flour, *divided*
  1/4 cup butter *or* margarine, softened
  1/4 cup shortening
    1 cup sugar
    2 eggs
  2/3 cup milk
  1/4 cup orange juice
    1 tablespoon baking powder
    1 teaspoon salt
  1/4 teaspoon ground cardamom

Combine candied fruit and 1 tablespoon flour in a small bowl; set aside. In a large mixing bowl, cream the butter, shortening and sugar for 1 minute. Add the eggs, milk, orange juice, baking powder, salt, cardamom and remaining flour. Beat on low speed for 30 seconds; beat on high for 3 minutes. Stir in fruit.

Pour into a greased and floured 9-in. x 5-in. x 3-in. loaf pan. Bake at 350° for 65-70 minutes or until a toothpick inserted near the center comes out clean. Cool for 10 minutes before removing from pan to a wire rack to cool completely. **Yield:** 1 loaf.

EASY MINT CHOCOLATE TRUFFLES
Jean Olson, Wallingford, Iowa

I make a lot of candy around the holidays. This is one of my favorites because the mixture isn't sticky or messy to work with, and the results are just delicious.

    1 tablespoon plus 3/4 cup butter (no substitutes), *divided*
    3 cups sugar
    1 can (5 ounces) evaporated milk
    2 cups (12 ounces) semisweet chocolate chips
  1/2 teaspoon peppermint extract
    1 jar (7 ounces) marshmallow creme
    1 teaspoon vanilla extract
Baking cocoa, finely chopped nuts *or* chocolate
    sprinkles

Line a 15-in. x 10-in. x 1-in. baking pan with foil. Grease the foil with 1 tablespoon butter; set aside. In a heavy saucepan, combine the sugar, milk and remaining butter. Bring to a boil over medium heat. Cook, stirring constantly, until a candy thermometer reads 234° (soft-ball stage). Remove from the heat; stir in chips and peppermint extract until chocolate is melted. Stir in marshmallow creme and vanilla until smooth. Spread into prepared pan.

Refrigerate, uncovered, for 3 hours or until firm. Lift out of pan; cut into 1-1/2-in. squares. Roll into 1-in. balls. Roll in cocoa, nuts or sprinkles. Refrigerate in an airtight container. **Yield:** 70 truffles.

Editor's Note: See the box on page 47 for information about testing your candy thermometer.

SPICY MIXED NUTS
Delores Hill, Helena, Montana

This different nut mix has an appealing kick, thanks to the cumin and chili powder I add. It's perfect for holiday snacking and gift giving.

    3 tablespoons butter *or* margarine
    1 pound mixed nuts
  1/4 teaspoon Worcestershire sauce
  1/2 teaspoon salt
  1/4 teaspoon paprika
  1/4 teaspoon cayenne pepper
  1/4 teaspoon chili powder
  1/8 teaspoon ground cumin

In a large skillet, melt butter. Add nuts and Worcestershire sauce; cook and stir over low heat for 5-7 minutes. Drain on paper towels. Place nuts in a large bowl. Combine seasonings; sprinkle over nuts and toss to coat. Cool. Store in an airtight container at room temperature. **Yield:** 3 cups.

MUSTARD CHEESE SPREAD
Lilburne Flohr-Svendsen, Barra Bonita, SP, Brazil

Wrapped up in a basket with crackers and a decorative spreader, this tangy cheese spread is a distinctive hostess gift. It's also good used as a dip for raw vegetables.

    1 package (8 ounces) cream cheese, softened
  1/2 cup butter *or* margarine, softened
    1 medium onion, finely chopped
    2 garlic cloves, minced
    2 to 3 tablespoons prepared mustard
    2 tablespoons paprika
  1/4 teaspoon salt
  1/8 teaspoon pepper
    1 tablespoon caraway seeds

In a mixing bowl, beat cream cheese and butter until smooth. Add the onion, garlic, mustard, paprika, salt and pepper. Spread onto an 8-in. serving platter; sprinkle with caraway seeds. Cover and refrigerate until serving. **Yield:** 2 cups.

BUTTERSCOTCH ICE CREAM TOPPING
Annie Gingerich, Greenwood, Wisconsin

Wonderful homemade goodness and true butterscotch flavor make this sweet rich sauce a well-enjoyed gift. We like it over ice cream or slices of pound cake. It reheats well in the microwave.

    1 cup packed brown sugar
  1/4 cup whipping cream
    3 tablespoons butter (no substitutes)
    2 tablespoons light corn syrup

In a heavy saucepan, combine all ingredients. Bring to a boil over medium heat; cook and stir for 3 minutes. Cool to room temperature. Cover and store in the refrigerator. To reheat, microwave at 50% power for 1 minute or until heated through. Serve warm over ice cream. **Yield:** 1-1/4 cups.

CRISPY COFFEE COOKIES
Romane Moeller, Colorado Springs, Colorado

I created this recipe because I wanted an easy-to-make cookie that folks can't resist. These tempting treats have a hint of coffee flavor and aren't overly sweet.

   1 cup sugar
  3/4 cup vegetable oil
  1/3 cup instant coffee granules
   2 tablespoons hot water
   2 eggs
2-1/2 cups all-purpose flour
1-1/2 teaspoons baking powder
  3/4 teaspoon salt
Additional sugar

In a mixing bowl, combine sugar and oil. Dissolve coffee in water; add to sugar mixture and mix well. Add eggs, one at a time, beating well after each addition. Combine the flour, baking powder and salt; gradually add to the sugar mixture.

Roll into 3/4-in. balls, then roll in additional sugar. Place 2 in. apart on lightly greased baking sheets; flatten with a fork. Bake at 400° for 8-10 minutes or until edges are firm. Remove to wire racks to cool. **Yield:** about 5 dozen.

ALMOND COFFEE CREAMER
Janet Lippincott, Akron, Ohio

This tasty creamer has just four simple ingredients—but its spicy almond flavor is so rich and soothing, friends will think you fussed. I give it in a holiday jar or with a Christmas mug.

3/4 cup confectioners' sugar
3/4 cup powdered nondairy creamer
  1 teaspoon ground cinnamon
  1 teaspoon almond extract

In a bowl, combine all the ingredients; mix well. Store in an airtight container. To use, add to coffee in place of nondairy creamer and sugar. **Yield:** 1-1/4 cups.

PECAN CARAMEL BARS
Trudy Schultz, Springfield, Missouri

These butterscotchy bars bring back fond memories of my grandma who loved to spoil us with good food. Whenever I give these treats away or take them to a buffet, folks request the recipe.

   2 cups all-purpose flour
   1 cup packed brown sugar
 1/2 cup cold butter (no substitutes)
1-1/2 cups pecan halves
   1 package (14 ounces) caramels
 1/4 cup whipping cream
   1 package (11-1/2 ounces) milk chocolate chips
   1 cup butterscotch chips

In a bowl, combine flour and brown sugar. Cut in butter until mixture is crumbly. Press into an ungreased 13-in. x 9-in. x 2-in. baking pan. Bake at 350° for 12-14 minutes or

until lightly browned. Cool on a wire rack. Sprinkle pecans over top.

In a microwave or heavy saucepan, melt caramels with cream; stir until smooth. Pour over pecans and spread evenly. Combine chocolate and butterscotch chips; spread over caramel layer. Bake 5 minutes longer. Remove to wire rack. Run a knife through melted chips to swirl; cool completely. Cut into bars. **Yield:** 2 dozen.

PEANUT BRITTLE BARS
Kristin Gleason, St. John, Kansas

Pairing the old-fashioned flavor of peanut brittle with yummy chocolate chips turns these bars into a satisfying treat and sought-after holiday gift.

1-1/2 cups all-purpose flour
 1/2 cup whole wheat flour
  1 cup packed brown sugar
  1 teaspoon baking soda
 1/4 teaspoon salt
  1 cup cold butter *or* margarine
TOPPING:
  2 cups salted peanuts
  1 cup milk chocolate chips
  1 jar (12-1/4 ounces) caramel ice cream topping
  3 tablespoons all-purpose flour

In a large bowl, combine flours, brown sugar, baking soda and salt. Cut in butter until mixture resembles coarse crumbs. Pat into a greased 15-in. x 10-in. x 1-in. baking pan. Bake at 350° for 10-12 minutes or until golden brown.

Sprinkle peanuts and chocolate chips over warm crust. Combine caramel topping and flour; drizzle over top. Bake 12-16 minutes longer or until golden brown and bubbly. Cool on a wire rack. Cut into squares. **Yield:** about 4 dozen.

GINGER SHORTBREAD WEDGES
Edna Hoffman, Hebron, Indiana

Rich, buttery and lightly spiced with ginger, this shortbread couldn't be tastier. Plus, since it uses pantry staples, it makes a handy last-minute gift.

1/2 cup butter (no substitutes), softened
1/3 cup sugar
  1 teaspoon ground ginger
  1 cup all-purpose flour

In a mixing bowl, cream the butter, sugar and ginger. Add flour; mix well (dough will be crumbly). Press dough into an ungreased 8-in. round baking pan. Using a fork, prick score lines to form eight wedges. Bake at 325° for 32-35 minutes or until edges are golden brown. Immediately cut into wedges along score marks. Cool in pan on a wire rack. **Yield:** 8 wedges.

> ● We recommend that you test your candy thermometer before each use by placing it in a pot of boiling water; the thermometer should read 212°. Adjust your recipe temperature up or down based on your test.

Candy Cane Chalet Will Sweeten Any Setting

THE CHEERY COTTAGE on our cover houses a very tasty secret. Instead of relying on the old-fashioned method of cutting out cookie dough to shape its walls, *CW*'s crafty kitchen staff turned to large candy bars for the chalet's construction!

"There's very little cutting involved. Mostly, you 'glue' the bars together with icing," details one of our home economists. "It couldn't be easier!"

Once the basic structure has been framed, you need only add the extras, including a candy cane roof and fence, a peppermint path and gumdrop greenery. So don't dwell on it anymore—begin building this confection-filled trim for your Christmas celebrations without delay!

CANDY CANE CHALET

ICING:
    12 cups confectioners' sugar, *divided*
     9 tablespoons meringue powder, *divided**
    18 tablespoons warm water, *divided*

CHALET AND ASSEMBLY:
     7 milk chocolate candy bars (7 ounces *each*)
    60 to 70 peppermint candy canes (5-1/2 inches long)
     9 large green gumdrops
     1 cream-filled strawberry wafer cookie
     3 red-hot candies

     1 miniature candy cane
     1 small green gumdrop
     1 small red gumdrop
    11 leaf-shaped spearmint gumdrops
Sugar
    11 starlight mints
     3 large red gumdrops
Pastry tips—round tip #5 and #2 and star tip #16 and #18
Pastry bags *or* heavy-duty resealable plastic bags
22-inch x 16-inch display base (cutting board, 1-inch-thick Styrofoam *or* piece of plywood covered with foil wrapping or aluminum foil)
Small cans for propping
Sharp knife
Serrated knife

***Editor's Note:** Meringue powder is available in cake and baking sections of many stores. It can also be ordered by mail from Wilton Industries, Inc., 2240 W. 75th St., Woodridge IL 60517; 1-800/794-5866. Or visit their Web site: *www.Wilton.com*.

To make icing: Prepare only one batch of icing at a time.

For each batch, in a large mixing bowl combine 4 cups confectioners' sugar, 3 tablespoons meringue powder and 6 tablespoons water. Beat on low speed for 7-10 minutes or until icing forms peaks. Place a damp cloth over the bowl and make sure to cover tightly between uses.

To assemble the frame of the chalet: Insert #5 tip into pastry bag and fill two-thirds full with icing. For chalet base, place one candy bar, smooth side up, on display board. Pipe a wide strip of icing close to the edges of the candy bar. Invert bar and position 2-1/2 in. from a short end of the display board.

Pipe icing along the long sides of the chocolate base. For each side of chalet, position a candy bar, smooth side out, and press firmly against the icing while holding base in place with one hand. Prop with small cans. (See Photo 1.) Pipe icing along the inside edges for added stability.

To assemble front and back of chalet: While sides of chalet are drying, trace house pattern on page 50 onto waxed paper, tagboard or thin cardboard and cut out.

Position the point of the pattern at one end of the smooth side of a candy bar. Using a sharp knife, lightly score long sides. Remove pattern. Using a serrated knife, carefully saw off the top two corners. Repeat with another candy bar.

Pipe icing along the short sides of the base and align the front and back chalet pieces, leaving a 1/4-in. gap between the inside edges of the candy bars. Press firmly together. Prop with small cans. Pipe icing along all outside edges for added stability; set aside to dry completely, about 4 hours. Remove cans.

To add side trim pieces: Cut 3-1/2-in. pieces from the straight end of eight candy canes; set aside curved ends for fence. Pipe icing into the gap at corners of chalet. Press straight candy canes onto icing on the inside and outside of all corners. Press canes together to secure. (See Photo 2.)

To make roof: Place one chocolate bar, smooth side up, on a flat surface. Pipe icing on outside edge of candy cane, stopping before the curve, and place on one end of the bar, making sure bottom of candy

Photo 1. Squeeze a strip of icing along the long side of the base. Position another candy bar perpendicular to base; press firmly into place and prop with cans until icing is dry.

Photo 2. Pipe icing into the gap in each corner. Position a straight candy cane on each side of the wall. Press candy canes together to secure.

Photo 3. Attach each candy cane with icing to smooth side of candy bar for roof.

cane is even with one side and curved end is up. Repeat 19 times, positioning candy canes so they line up straight. (See Photo 3.) Repeat for other side of roof. Set aside to dry completely, about 4 hours.

Cut 4 in. from the straight end of four candy canes; set aside curved pieces for fence. Pipe icing along the top edge of one side of the chalet. Carefully position a roof piece in place. Immediately pipe icing between the roof piece and the roof edge at the front of chalet. Press a straight candy cane piece into icing;

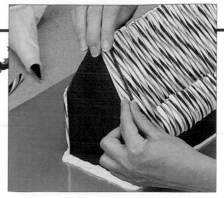

Photo 4. Place one roof piece in position, then pipe icing along the slanted roofline and place a straight candy cane piece over icing. Hold in place until set, about 1 minute.

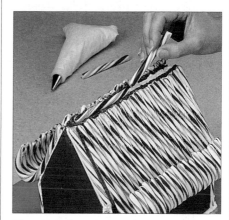

Photo 5. Pipe icing along peak of the roof. Insert two straight candy canes into gap.

Photo 6. Dab icing onto the bottom of the spearmint pieces and place additional pieces above gaps in the previous layer for trees.

hold firmly until set, about 1 minute. (See Photo 4.)

Repeat for back of chalet. Repeat with second roof piece and two remaining straight candy cane pieces.

Cut two candy canes into 3-1/2- in. straight pieces. Reserve curved tops for fence. Pipe icing along crevice in roof top. Insert the straight candy cane pieces for stability. (See Photo 5.) Let dry completely, about 4 hours.

To make windows and doors: Cut 1/8 in. from the bottom of five large green gumdrops; set tops aside for

(Instructions continue on next page)

bushes. Using a #2 tip, decorate cut side of gumdrops with lines for window panes. With a dab of icing, attach windows to front and sides of chalet, positioning as shown in photo.

For door, cut wafer cookie to 2-1/2 in. x 1-1/4 in. Attach to front of chalet with icing. Position one red-hot with icing for doorknob.

Cut one 2-in. straight piece and two 2-1/2-in. straight pieces from three candy canes; position around top and sides of door with icing. Cap ends of door mantle with red-hots.

Cut three 4-in. straight pieces from candy canes; set aside curved tops for fence. Attach the straight pieces with icing to the front of the chalet above the door, forming a triangle along the roof peak.

To make lamppost and trees: For the lamppost, gently insert bottom of miniature candy cane into small green gumdrop. Gently push a small red gumdrop into the curved end for the light; set aside.

Each tree uses 2-1/2 leaf-shaped spearmint gumdrops. Cut the top half off one leaf gumdrop; set aside for tree top. Cut remaining portion in half lengthwise, forming two triangles.

Place bottoms of triangles together, forming tree base. Cut remaining two leaf gumdrops in half lengthwise, then cut each half into quarters. Dip all cut sides of gumdrops in sugar. Pinch ends of each piece to exaggerate the tip.

Pipe icing onto tree base; arrange four gumdrop pieces, with tips pointing out and edges touching, over base. Repeat twice, positioning above the open spaces of the layer below. (See photo 6 on previous page.) Add the reserved tree top. Press pieces firmly together, repositioning pieces if necessary. Repeat for additional trees. Set aside to dry, about 1 hour.

Add finishing touches: Working in small sections, frost base with icing for snow. Trim ends of 12 reserved

candy cane curves so they will sit level; insert curves into icing until the fence is the desired length.

Use nine starlight mints for path. Position trees and lamppost as desired. Use reserved cut gumdrops from the windows and remaining leaf gumdrop for bushes on the sides of the chalet.

Pipe icing on the bottoms of large red and remaining green gumdrops and position along roof top. Add starlight mints to ends of roof.

Using #16 star tip, pipe icing stars along the roof seam at the front and back of the chalet. Using #18 star tip, pipe icing icicles on each side of roof peak, tree and shrubs.

Enjoy your candy-coated creation!

Under Construction

Here are some handy hints sure to make raising your chalet a cinch:

- Double-check candy bars at the store to make sure they aren't broken.
- When cutting off corners of candy bars for the roof pieces, use a gentle sawing motion with a serrated knife.
- Use a serrated knife to trim candy cane pieces. An emery board works nicely to "file" away any rough edges.
- While the side pieces of the chalet are drying, go ahead and start "gluing" the candy canes to the roof pieces. You can also cut the spearmint leaves and assemble the trees ahead of time.
- When arranging the candy canes, be sure the spiral on each is twisting in the same direction.
- Leftover candy cane pieces can be crushed and stirred into hot chocolate, sprinkled over ice cream or added to your favorite sugar cookie dough.
- Since manufacturers make many different sizes of candy canes, the chalet design may need to be adjusted accordingly, depending on the kind you can find.

**CANDY CANE CHALET
HOUSE PATTERN**
Cut 2—chocolate bars

Grandma's 'Brag' Page

SANTA-SHY. Upon sighting a jolly gent in red, Katie Marie can't believe her eyes. Grandma Lillian Gallagher says she's a whisker away from warming up to him in Whitehorse, Yukon Territory.

MAKING *MMM*ERRY. Granddaughter Taylor, age 6, really got into baking at Mary Pauley's house in Lloyd, Kentucky. "She got as much sugar and flour on herself as she did in her goodies!"

FIDDLING AROUND for this Christmas card cover, Kelli LeClaire earned her wings. "At 18 months, she's indeed a little angel," proclaims Grandma Barb Nelson of Williams, Minnesota.

JOY TO HER WORLD is what a house full of grandchildren brings to Kathy Clark from Raleigh, North Carolina. "During a cousins' play day, we posed them in costume around a manger scene for a Christmas picture I'll always cherish," she says of cheery cherubs, ranging in age from 9 to 2.

CAPPING CHRISTMAS with a fashion show are Andrew, Morgan, Jordan and Melissa, modeling pj's and hats Grandma Helen Nicholson stitched in Oakville, Ontario.

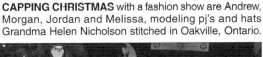

Nature's Photography

ELF-CONFIDENT in his holiday-style outfit, Jeannine Manuel's great-grandson Brendan Bachmeier (left) is well-suited to Yuletide. She sent snap of Santa's sidekick from Fairfield, Montana.

51

Country Decorating...

Happy Snowmen Melt Hearts In Every Room of Her House!

WHEN it comes to Christmas, Anne Krystyniak's motto is "Let it snow, let it snow, let it snow"!

As December draws near and those first fluffy flakes fill the air, she rings in the season with snowmen. But Anne doesn't have to brave the cold to roll out frozen figures. She just pulls them from eight giant plastic storage boxes.

The Watertown, Wisconsin wife has amassed a collection that numbers close to 600. And that doesn't include the trims you might find on her Christmas tree.

On a white November day, there's a flurry of activity in the Krystyniak home as Anne places snowmen of all shapes and sizes on windowsills and shelves. They're lined up on the mantel, tucked in wreaths, grouped on the floor, seated in chairs, hung on walls and dangled from curtains.

It takes about three days to complete her seasonal setup. And the frosty fellows are absolutely everywhere.

Anne sets the mood with a wooden plaque hung under the front porch light that proclaims "Snowmen Gather Here". Skinny wooden sentinels stand watch by the door, and snowman bulbs light the landscape.

Inside, the living room is snowed under with spirit. A 5-foot soft-sculptured gent slouches in a rocking chair. Fanciful figurines, coasters, tins and candy dishes—all touting the jolly soul—adorn tables. And a snowman painted on a hanging windowpane basks in the sun.

On the powder room mirror, a spirited self-sticking snowman smiles happily at all who see him, while snowman-shaped bottles hold powder and lotion. Nearby, a frosty wall hanging twinkles with pretty lights.

The seasonal charmers also grin from atop the refrigerator, the microwave and the kitchen counters and hang from a ceiling light fixture. A pudgy snowman cookie jar props up a row of cookbooks.

Snowmen finally drift to the basement rec room, where every corner is soon billowing with the cheery chaps.

Anne's collection is a melting pot, born from ceramic, gourds, tin, wood, fabric—almost anything you can think of. They wear top hats, knit caps and earmuffs, shawls, scarves and Santa suits. Some hold lights, brooms or blocks. Others perch in wheelbarrows or wagons.

A bowling pin snowman sports a snappy green vest. One fuzzy character in a straw hat and Hawaiian shirt declares "Think Spring". And a whimsical draft dodger sprawls out by the door, protecting the house from winter's chill.

This menagerie didn't materialize overnight. Anne has been stocking up for over 20 years, with help from husband Bob.

"Bob and I love to shop," Anne says. "We decided it would be fun to collect something."

So, they set their sights on snowmen—and it snowballed.

Anne doesn't have a favorite. There are far too many to choose from. "I enjoy the odd ones in particular, like the starfish, the antique toothbrush and the antique rattle," she admits, "but I honestly like them all."

Incredibly, Anne has only one duplicate—she and Bob each bought the same

FROSTY FACES gather on shelves and on floors (top) in Anne Krystyniak's home. One jolly fellow blocks the cold (above), and others welcome holiday guests (below left).

crafty wooden fence with snowmen and trees within hours of each other.

Every Christmas, the couple's cat, "Buddy", and golden retriever, "Ace", have to share their turf with this flock of spritely fellows and unusual accessories. But they have warmed up to the snowmen just fine.

"Ace just goes with the flow," Anne laughs, "but the cat has to check them all out. He walks around them on the basement ledge and the tables."

Despite a few bumps, there have been no pet-inflicted bruises to the growing snowman family.

And growing it is. Anne still acquires about 20 a year. Some are gifts, while others are souvenirs. The couple recently brought back their first European additions from Italy and Holland. Not

SNAPPY SNOWMEN stand out in the Krystyniaks' three-season room (top), populate the powder room (above) and ledges (right). Anne and husband Bob (above right) have been collecting the frozen fellows for over 20 years.

any snowman will do, however.

"I am particular about what I pick up," Anne explains. "No expensive limited edition ones and nothing too cutesy.

"When I started collecting, snowmen weren't popular. Now, they're everywhere—and I love it! I just can't get enough of those roly-poly fellows."

I'll Never Forget...

Mom and Dad Found All Sorts Of Ways to Make Yuletide Fun

By Jerri Ainsworth of Markle, Indiana

I AM AMAZED every time I reminisce about past Christmases. My brother, sister and I had plenty of good times together each December…all thanks to our parents' active imaginations!

Mom and Dad, as I now know, were always up to something. We didn't know it, but *they* engineered the sightings of Santa and his reindeer and the telephone calls that came directly from the jolly old elf himself. We kids just felt very fortunate that Santa found time for us in his busy schedule.

We'd also make our own fun, like the time we set a trap in the doorway for Kris Kringle on Christmas Eve, just so we could catch him and talk to him in the morning.

When we clambered out of bed shortly after sunrise the next day, we were greeted with evidence that somehow that crafty Claus had managed to escape our snare—one of his black boots along with a few white whiskers were all he'd left behind.

We were absolutely shocked that our little trick had almost worked…and ashamed that we'd made him deliver toys and packages to the rest of the world wearing only one boot.

His chin must have hurt, too, we reasoned after examining the whiskers left in the trap. I felt so guilty, I penned an apology for our unruly antics.

Wrapping Up a Surprise

One of my favorite recollections is the year Mom and the three of us decided to stump Dad. Somehow, our father seemed to know what kind of gift Mom had gotten him each year before he'd removed any of the wrapping paper.

We never did without necessities, but money was very tight, so most presents were on the practical side. That year, Mom had purchased a much-needed crowbar and had us package it.

While we were busy, she hauled in the most enormous box we'd ever seen. It took up the whole end of our living room!

After we finished with the crowbar, the four of us decorated the big box. For a final touch, we tacked on a tag that read "To: Dad/From: Mom".

The plan was to put the wrapped tool in the big box so Dad couldn't possibly guess what it was. We were so excited we could hardly contain ourselves!

It was hard not to spoil the surprise—Christmas seemed so far away. The normal anticipation the holiday conjured up was magnified by the thought of playing this little trick on Dad.

I remember, too, being fascinated with the box itself. What fun it would be to turn it into a playhouse! Instead, I stayed as far away as I could so I would not let the cat out of the bag.

Finally, December 25 arrived. The stockings were full and presents were piled up under the tree. Of course, we wanted Dad to unwrap the big box first, but tradition dictated otherwise. So we kids opened our gifts, then Mom opened hers…and then it was Dad's turn.

In the Know

We watched him exclaim over packages from under the tree, growing more and more giddy as he got closer to opening the huge box. Then it was time!

We all gathered around and cheered Dad on as he carefully examined the box, announcing that he knew it was the tractor cab he'd been wanting. Boy, was he going to be surprised!

Slowly, he started to peel back the paper. Then, to our amazement, he lifted the huge box up and revealed something we never expected—a beautiful, brand-new Wurlitzer piano. And sitting on the bench was the wrapped-up crowbar.

At a total loss for words, my siblings and I just stared. In a moment, though, the silence was broken by our whoops of joy—we were elated!

To this day, I can't believe the three of us kids never looked behind the box. The piano had been delivered while we were at school…and all along the real plan had been for Mom and Dad to surprise *us*.

It wasn't until I had children of my own that I understood how much fun my parents had at Christmas. The delight I take in making memories for my offspring is so much more rewarding than any gift I might receive.

I know that's how Dad felt the year he discovered something other than a tractor cab under the tree!

To: Dad
From: Mom

Claus Crafter Adds Character To Any Christmas Celebration!

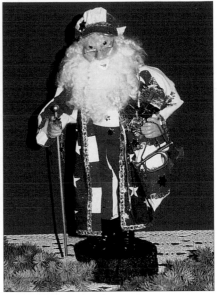

NICKS OF TIME. Shirley Pensak's sculpted and stitched Kris Kringles range from old-world Santas to Victorian St. Nicks to contemporary Clauses. And no two are alike!

A KNACK for making St. Nick gives Shirley Pensak a sack full of reasons for celebrating in style. The Saylorsburg, Pennsylvania crafter is busy as an elf herself, sculpting and stitching Santas year-round!

"Santa means so much to me," relates Shirley. "He embodies all the old notions of Christmas—hope, laughter, family, traditions and memories.

"My godfather, Tom Evans, donned the red suit and merry disposition each year at our local VFW. He brought so much joy and good cheer. I try to capture that in my Santas."

Sewing up the task is a year-round adventure for her whole family. "Our daughters—Patty, Susan and Lorrie—help me hunt for Santa garb at auctions, yard sales and bargain stores.

"Old fur coats and stoles, vintage clothing, wool sweaters and blankets are all on the list. Secondhand leather purses carry lots of potential for boots and belts, while pretty buttons and baubles come in handy in all sorts of ways," she explains.

While the women search for suitable materials, the men focus on the foundations. "My son-in-law, Roger, cuts platforms for my Santas from walnut boards. Then they're sanded and varnished by husband Edward."

Come fall, Shirley's workshop is well stocked, and she's ready to start constructing her one-of-a-kind Christmas characters.

"I use a heavy-duty wire for the arms and legs," she offers. "The body is stuffed with muslin and dressed using the furs, sweaters and other materials we've gathered.

"I sculpt the faces out of clay last, when I have a pretty clear picture of Santa's personality. That's important because I want each one to tell his own story. Lastly, I add sheep's wool for hair and a beard.

"The whole process takes 4-6 hours for a simple Santa and about a day for a more complex one," notes Shirley.

By the time Shirley's done, these 8-inch or larger figures are packed with personality. They range from old-world Kringles to folksy fellows, Victorian gents and modern models.

"My Santas play baseball, golf, fish, farm and fiddle. I've made ethnic versions and anything else that strikes my fancy," she smiles. "No two figures are ever alike."

To date, she's handcrafted over 300. "Most sell by word of mouth," comments Shirley, who only attends one craft show a year. "People see them and are drawn to their faces.

"Maybe they see how much my Santas mean to me, how much care I take in crafting them. What *I* treasure are the expressions I see when folks find a Kringle that suits their style."

Editor's Note: *For more information on Shirlee's Santas, send a self-addressed stamped envelope to Shirley Pensak, R.D. 1, Box 1512, Saylorsburg PA 18353.*

Robert Ranney

Creativity Is Stirring All Throughout Her House!

WALL-TO-WALL hospitality is a Christmas tradition for Susan Larberg. The cordial Floridian convinces hundreds of visitors that there's no place like home for a holiday craft show.

"People welcome the chance to attend a cozy open house and go holiday shopping all at once," Susan says with a smile. Her home boutique in rural Brooksville opens the door to rooms full of handcrafts made by her and other members of her family.

"The first year, I invited a few friends and neighbors to see our Christmas crafts exhibited on the dining room table," she recalls. "It was such a hit, we've been doing it every season since, displaying accents from the floor to the rafters!"

Upon arriving, guests from several surrounding counties are greeted at the doorstep with merry music and cheery outdoor decor. Hostess Susan invites them to browse all around the house—each area features a different theme.

"The extra bedroom is filled with garden crafts and stuffed animals, and the bathroom has every seashell accent imaginable," Susan points out.

"Country furniture and decorated sleighs are set up in the great room, and the dining room has cherubs gracing frames, centerpieces, plaques and wall hangings.

"To create a festive atmosphere, I trimmed 16 trees of various shapes and sizes and strung small white lights across shelves, doorways, windows and kitchen cabinets. With the fireplace crackling and the aroma of cookies in the air, it's almost impossible not to get into the Christmas spirit."

There's clearly no shortage of Yule enthusiasm in her creative clan, Susan affirms. "My brother, Chris, makes beautiful pine shelves, quilt racks and tables, Dad builds birdhouses and Mom fashions 4-foot foam lollipops.

"My husband, Dennis, assembles old-fashioned lanterns and our grown daughters, Jennifer and Stacey, make angels."

The flurry of activity lasts from the boutique's opening the weekend before Thanksgiving to the second weekend in December. "We're all ready for a rest by then," Susan chuckles.

"But by spring, we're planning how to transform the house into a holiday wonderland again."

Editor's Note: *Susan's Christmas Boutique opens November 15-19 and continues on Saturdays and Sundays until December 9. For exact times and directions, send a self-addressed stamped envelope to Golden Touch Crafts, 27271 Hickory Hill Rd., Brooksville FL 34602-8257 or call 1-352/796-7522.* 🔔

HOLIDAY HOUSE that Susan Larberg (above left) opens to the public showcases her family's homespun crafts in seasonal splendor.

'House' Your Own Craft Show

If you're ready to host your own boutique, crafter Susan Larberg suggests:

● Start decorating early. "Usually, Dennis and I begin setting up shelves and moving out furniture on October 1."

● Offer a variety of unique homemade items and display them tastefully in various rooms. "Even our kitchen is loaded with products, from gourmet gift baskets and flavored vinegar and oil to silk fruit and flower baskets and swags."

● Spread the word. "I distribute colorful flyers to local businesses, friends and neighbors and mail them to previous customers."

● Make your guests feel welcome. "We invite them to visit the kitchen for oven-fresh cookies, coffee, tea and punch."

● Look into local ordinances. "Check for regulations concerning zoning, selling food, etc. before organizing a home boutique."

The Holidays Are a Time This Crafter Bears in Mind

AS December 25th approaches, it's obvious…Betty Lisk of rural Elizabeth, Illinois has a beary merry Christmas all sewn up.

"Real bears hibernate in winter—but this is when *my* furry friends come out to play," Betty relates from her home-based craft studio and shop.

About now, the cuddly stuffed bruins she produces fill every room and nearly all *her* waking hours.

Since opening her den of delights 6 years ago, Betty has typically turned out 250 teddies a year. Her cute cast of characters varies from 10 to 36 inches tall and sports coats of mohair, synthetic and recycled fur, chenille and other scrappy fabrics.

"At Christmas, my bears have a holiday flair," Betty cheerily declares. "I fashion them into angels, elves, Mr. and Mrs. Claus, polar bears and snowmen. Many wear vests or dresses of velvet and satin. Why, I've even dyed their fur red and green.

"I stitch most all of their clothing," she adds, sewing a jingling bell onto a dapper Santa's cap. Betty regularly makes bear tracks to flea markets and rummage sales, hunting for wire-rimmed glasses, lace collars, shoe buckles, buttons and such.

Customers provide the "ins-bear-ation" for many of her homemade buddies, Betty warmly informs. "Often they'll bring me a well-worn coat or a quilt they just can't bear to part with—and I have the makings for a family heirloom bear.

"Others request teddies depicting a profession, hobby or heritage. I've constructed bear farmers and teachers, bingo players and fishermen…even a Dutch bear complete with wooden shoes."

You don't have to be a child to have a soft spot for fuzzy faces, Betty amiably attests. "Adults purchase my jointed bears as collectibles to cozy up their furniture and shelves. For youngsters, I make squeezable critters with no detachable parts. They're very good at calming fears and keeping secrets."

As word about her gentle teddies spreads, mail orders are coming in from across the country. "Still, my husband, John, and I enjoy it most when customers visit our home," Betty confirms.

"That way, they can meet my bears in person and see just how loving, understanding and huggable they are."

And considering the charm of Betty's old-fashioned friends, anybody would be pleased to receive the bear necessities as a gift for Christmas or any time of year.

Editor's Note: *To receive a brochure about her homemade bears, send a self-addressed stamped envelope to Betty Lisk, 215 S. Main St., Box 166, Elizabeth IL 61028, or call her at 1-815/858-3343.* 🔔

GRIN AND BEAR IT. Betty Lisk's cute and cuddly critters are sure to put a smile on anyone's face, young or old. And this time of year, the merry bears are dolled up for the holidays.

tered onto wrong side of 4-in. x 6-in. piece of bandanna fabric following manufacturer's directions. Remove paper backing and, with edges matching, fuse to wrong side of same size piece of off-white fabric.

Place wing pattern on fused fabrics with grain lines matching. Trace around pattern. Remove pattern. Cut out wings just inside traced lines.

Press a narrow hem to wrong side of all sides of 12-in. square of bandanna fabric for skirt. Sew hem in place with matching thread.

Fold skirt in half diagonally with wrong sides together to make a triangle with fold on top (see Fig. 1a). Press fold. Fold opposite ends of triangle in to make a square (see Figs. 1b and 1c). Folds will be in back of skirt.

To attach head, insert top (corner with folds) into opening of wooden bead or ball (see Fig. 2). Push corner of fabric through bead or ball until about 1/4 in. of fabric extends through on the other side. Glue as needed to hold. Let dry.

Glue lengths of yarn centered over top of head. Separate yarn at each side of head into three groups and make a braid at each side. Tie thread around braids about 1 in. from ends to hold. Trim ends of braids to desired length.

Glue hat onto top of head.

Cut a 12-in. length of ribbon. Wrap

Colorful Cowgirl Angels Round Up Yuletide Spirit

REINING IN just the right trim was an easy chore for Jan Koepsell. "It's typical for folks around here to decorate trees with a ranch theme," she pens from Paonia, Colorado.

"That inspired me to create these cowgirl angels, complete with bandanna outfits, mini straw hats and homespun wings."

You don't need to live out West to make them, though. The high-flying Christmas figures will fit fine into any country decor!

Materials Needed (for one):
Pattern on next page
Tracing paper and pencil
3-inch x 5-inch piece of paper-backed fusible web
100% cotton or cotton-blend fabrics—12-inch square and 4-inch x 6-inch piece of red bandanna print, and 4-inch x 6-inch

piece of off-white solid (Jan used homespun fabric)
Matching all-purpose thread
1-1/4-inch natural round wooden bead or ball with center hole for head
Thirty-six 9-inch-long strands of 2-ply tan yarn for hair
Straw hat to fit head
24 inches of 1/8-inch-wide red satin ribbon
Fine-line permanent markers—brown and red
Glue gun and glue stick or white (tacky) glue
Standard sewing supplies

Finished Size: Angel measures about 5 inches across x 9 inches tall.

Directions:
Trace wing pattern onto folded tracing paper. Cut out on traced lines and open for complete pattern.

Fuse paper-backed fusible web cen-

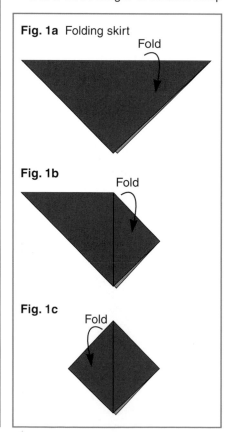

Fig. 1a Folding skirt
Fold

Fig. 1b
Fold

Fig. 1c
Fold

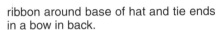

ribbon around base of hat and tie ends in a bow in back.

Cut remaining length of ribbon in half. Wrap each half over thread at ends of braids. Tie ribbons in a knot. Trim ends to desired length.

Use markers to add two small brown dots for eyes and small red dot for nose as shown in photo.

Referring to photo for placement, glue off-white side of wings centered onto back of angel.

Attach a loop of thread to top of hat for hanger. ♛

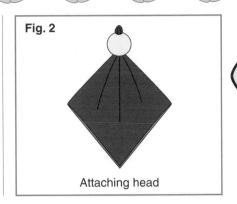

Fig. 2

Attaching head

BANDANNA ANGEL PATTERN WING
Trace 1—folded tracing paper
Cut 1—as directed

Grain

Foldline

Easy-to-Stitch Afghan Has Season Covered

NEVER mind Jack Frost when this comfy country blanket is nearby. It's perfect for chasing away those winter chills this Christmas…and beyond.

Renee Dent of Conrad, Montana created the soothing spread with easy-to-find worsted-weight yarn and stitches so simple, it's a cinch to crochet. You can quickly bundle your home in holiday hues, then work up another for someone you love.

Materials Needed:
4-ply worsted weight yarn—four 8-ounce skeins of red and two 3.5-ounce skeins each of green and white (Renee used Coats and Clark Red Heart yarn No. 390 Hot Red, No. 368 Paddy Green and No. 311 White)
Size N/15 (10mm) crochet hook
Size 13 tapestry needle
Scissors

Finished Size: Afghan is about 35 inches wide x 48 inches long.

Directions:
Working with two strands of red yarn as one, ch 74. (Loop on hook does not count as a ch.)

Row 1: Sk first two chs; * sc in next ch, hdc in next ch, sk 1 ch; repeat from * across row, ending with hdc in last ch, turn.

Row 2: Ch 2; * sk hdc, work 1 sc and 1 hdc in next sc; repeat from * across row, ending with hdc in last ch, turn.

Repeat Row 2 until afghan is about 45 in. long. Fasten off at end of last row.

EDGING: Round 1: Working with two strands of white yarn as one, attach yarn with a sl st in corner; * work 3 scs in same sp; work scs evenly spaced along side of afghan to next corner; work 3 scs in the corner; work scs evenly spaced across end of afghan to next corner; repeat from * around, join with a sl st in beginning st.

Round 2: Repeat Round 1, working 1 sc in each sc and working 3 scs in center sc of each corner. Fasten off.

Round 3: Working with two strands of green yarn as one, attach yarn with a sl st in any corner, repeat Round 2. Fasten off.

FINISHING: Use tapestry needle to weave in all loose ends. ♛

ABBREVIATIONS

ch(s)	chain(s)
hdc(s)	half double crochet(s)
sc(s)	single crochet(s)
sk	skip
sl st	slip stitch
sp	space
*	Instructions following asterisk are repeated as instructed.

Sleigh Centerpiece Makes Tables Bright!

WANT to add a dash of Christmas cheer to your home? The North Pole pleaser shown here will do the trick. It's sure to ring in the season whether you top a table with it, line a mantel or bring it to a stop amid a buffet!

Rather than paint the wood sleigh, Maurine Henry decoupaged pieces of fabric to enliven the sides.

"The reindeer aren't just decorative," she points out from Keene, New Hampshire. "They can hold napkins or holiday greetings as well."

Materials Needed:
Patterns on next page
Tracing paper and pencil
Graphite paper
Stylus or dry ballpoint pen
32-inch length of 1 x 8 pine lumber for sleigh (actual size is about 3/4 inch x 7-1/4 inches)
30-inch length of 1 x 6 pine lumber for reindeer (actual size is about 3/4 inch x 5-1/2 inches)
Scroll or band saw
Table saw (optional)
1-inch hole saw
Drill with 1/4-inch and 1/16-inch bits
Sandpaper and tack cloth
Light brown wood stain and soft cloth
Paper plate or palette
Acrylic craft paints—black and off-white
Paintbrushes—small flat, small round, liner and small sponge brush
Clear acrylic spray sealer
1-1/2-inch finishing nails
Hammer

Wood glue
Two 6-inch x 12-inch pieces of red Christmas print fabric
Decoupage finish
1/8-inch-wide satin ribbon—1/2 yard of green and 2-1/2 yards of red
Floral foam
Several artificial holly picks
Scissors

Finished Size: Sleigh is 11 inches long x 6-1/2 inches high x 4-1/2 inches wide. Each reindeer is about 5 inches high x 4-1/2 inches long x 3/4 inch thick.

Directions:
SLEIGH: Use copy machine to enlarge pattern to 200%, or mark tracing paper with a 1-in. grid and draw pattern as shown onto tracing paper.

Place sleigh pattern on 1 x 8 pine with grain lines matching. Slip a piece of graphite paper between pattern and wood. Trace over pattern lines with stylus or dry ballpoint pen to transfer pattern onto wood. Repeat.

Use scroll or band saw to cut around outline of each side of sleigh. For sleigh runners, first drill a hole through cutout areas. Then insert blade of saw through holes and cut out each shaded space.

From 1 x 8 pine, also cut one 3-in. x 3-7/8-in. piece for back, one 3-in. x 3-1/2-in. piece for front and one 3-in. x 3-5/8-in. piece for bottom of sleigh.

If desired, use table saw to cut one 3-in. edge of the front piece at a 30° angle and one 3-in. edge of the back piece at a 15° angle.

Sand pieces smooth and wipe with

tack cloth to remove sanding dust. Use soft cloth to apply stain to all sides of pieces. Let dry.

ASSEMBLY: Glue short edges of front, back and bottom together to form center of sleigh. Let dry.

Center sleigh sides along sides of sleigh bottom with bottom of sleigh just above runner cutouts. Pre-drill holes with 1/16-in. bit to prevent splitting. Then attach sides with finishing nails.

Spray with sealer. Let dry.

Decoupage: Cut top of sleigh pattern from runners on dashed line of pattern. Cut two sleigh tops from Christmas print as directed on pattern.

Use sponge brush to apply decoupage finish to one side of sleigh. Place sleigh fabric right side out over wet decoupage finish with edges matching. Smooth to remove bubbles. Trim edges even with sleigh if needed. Let dry.

Apply another coat of decoupage finish over fabric. Place a piece of green ribbon along lower edge of sleigh fabric. Cut ends even with sleigh. Apply decoupage finish over ribbon. Let dry. Repeat on other side of sleigh.

REINDEER: Trace reindeer pattern onto tracing paper. Then place pattern on 1 x 6 pine with grain lines matching. Slip a piece of graphite paper between pattern and wood. Trace over pattern with stylus or dry ballpoint pen. Repeat five more times.

Use scroll or band saw to cut around outlines of each reindeer. Use hole saw to cut 1-in. hole through each where indicated on pattern.

Sand pieces smooth and wipe with

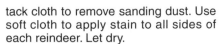

tack cloth to remove sanding dust. Use soft cloth to apply stain to all sides of each reindeer. Let dry.

Painting: Place small amounts of paints as needed onto paper plate or palette. Apply additional coats of paint as needed for complete coverage, allowing drying time between coats.

Paint both sides of each reindeer the same and extend paint onto the front of each.

Use small flat brush to fill in off-white areas as shown on pattern. Let dry.

Use round brush and black to paint noses, eyes and centers of ears.

Use liner to add off-white highlights to eyes and black detail lines as shown on pattern. Let dry.

FINISHING: Cut floral foam to fit inside sleigh. Add holly picks to fill sleigh as shown in photo.

Cut six 15-in.-long pieces of red ribbon. Tie a ribbon around the neck of each reindeer.

Position reindeer in front of sleigh as desired. Or place napkins in holes of reindeer and use reindeer for napkin rings.

Slide your sleigh and reindeer set onto a table!

SLEIGH SIDE

Trace 1—tracing paper
Cut 2—1 x 8 pine
Cut 2, reversing 1 as directed—
Christmas print

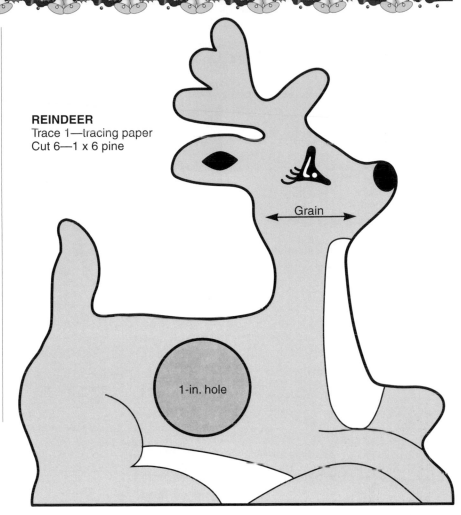

REINDEER
Trace 1—tracing paper
Cut 6—1 x 6 pine

Grain

1-in. hole

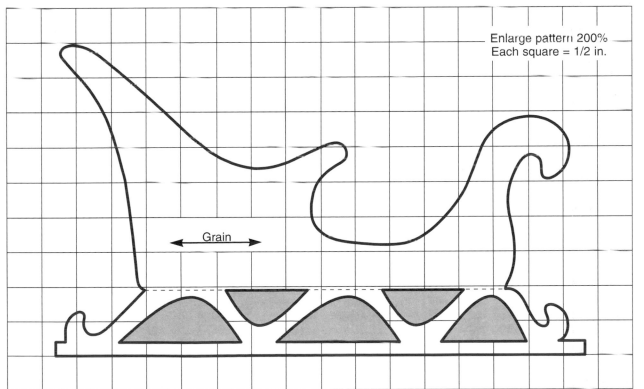

Enlarge pattern 200%
Each square = 1/2 in.

Grain

Snowy Garland Wraps Up Christmas

WHETHER you string them along a mantel or swirl these frosty fellows around a door frame, you're sure to add more than a dusting of hearty fun to the festivities!

Created by crafter Patricia Schroedl of Jefferson, Wisconsin, the garland features easy-to-paint wooden figures and hearts. "Felt strips serve as scarves, and wire pieces form arms for the snowmen," she describes.

Want a longer version? Simply add as many snowmen and hearts as you like.

Materials Needed:
Patterns on this page
Tracing paper and pencil
30 inches of 4-inch-wide x 1/4-inch-thick basswood
Scroll saw
Drill with 1/8-inch bit
Sandpaper and tack cloth
Water basin
Paper towels
Newspapers
Paper plate or palette
Acrylic craft paints—black, light blue-green, dark green, orange, dark red and white
Textured snow paint
Paintbrushes—small flat, small round, liner, old scruffy brush and spatter brush or old toothbrush
Clear acrylic spray sealer
Eight 4-inch-long pieces of black 20-gauge craft wire

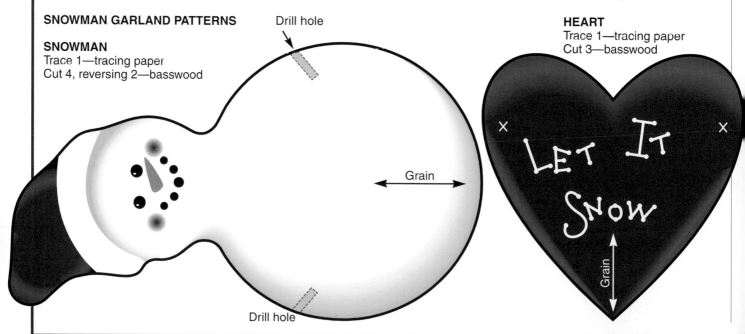

Eight 18-inch-long pieces of 2-ply jute string
1/2-inch wooden beads—16 natural and eight each of green and red
Four 1/4-inch wooden balls or beads for tips of hats
Four 8-inch-long x 1/2-inch-wide strips of red felt for scarves
White (tacky) glue
Scissors

Finished Size: The garland measures about 45 inches long x 5 inches high.

Directions:
CUTTING: Trace patterns onto tracing paper. Cut out each on traced lines.

With the grain lines matching, trace around heart pattern onto basswood three times.

With grain lines matching, trace around snowman pattern onto basswood twice. Reverse pattern and trace around snowman onto basswood two more times.

Cut out shapes using scroll saw. Drill holes into sides of each snowman where indicated on pattern. Drill holes through hearts at each "X" on pattern.

Sand smooth and wipe with tack cloth to remove sanding dust.

Glue a 1/4-in. wooden ball or bead to tip of each snowman's hat. Let dry.

PAINTING: Place small amounts of paints onto paper plate or palette as needed. Paint each piece as directed,

SNOWMAN GARLAND PATTERNS

SNOWMAN
Trace 1—tracing paper
Cut 4, reversing 2—basswood

Drill hole

Grain

Drill hole

HEART
Trace 1—tracing paper
Cut 3—basswood

x   x

LET IT SNOW

Grain

extending paint onto edges of each. Apply additional coats of paint as needed for complete coverage, allowing drying time between coats.

Use flat brush and white to paint each snowman. While paint is still wet, use flat brush and light blue-green to shade the top of each snowman's head and edge of each body as shown on pattern. Let dry.

Use flat brush to paint one snowman hat dark red, one light blue-green, one dark green and one black. While paint is wet, use black to shade edges of hats (except black hat). Let dry.

Dip handle of paintbrush into black paint and add small dots for eyes and mouth to each snowman. Let dry.

Use round brush and orange paint to add a carrot nose to each. Let dry.

Dip flat brush into dark red paint and wipe off excess onto paper towel until brush is nearly dry. Use a circular motion to add cheeks to each snowman. Let dry.

Dip handle of brush into white and dab tiny highlights onto each eye.

Use old scruffy brush to apply snow texture paint to band and tip of each snowman's hat. Let dry.

Use flat brush and dark red to paint each heart. While paint is still wet, use flat brush and black to shade outer edge of each heart. Let dry.

Thin white paint with a bit of water and use liner to add lettering to each heart as shown on pattern. Let dry.

Place painted pieces on newspaper to protect surfaces around and underneath them.

Mix equal parts of white paint and water. Using spatter brush or old toothbrush, dip brush into thinned paint. Hold bristles toward piece about 8 in. from area to be spattered and pull another brush handle or your finger across bristles. Repeat, spattering each piece as desired. Let dry.

Spray hearts and snowmen with sealer. Let dry.

ASSEMBLY: Fold piece of craft wire in half. Insert pencil at fold of wire and wrap ends together to twist, leaving 1/2

in. from fold untwisted. Repeat with remaining pieces of craft wire, making eight wire arms.

Dip twisted ends of an arm into glue and insert ends into a drilled hole on snowman. Repeat with remaining pieces of twisted wire, adding arms to each snowman.

Thread a piece of jute string through one hole of one heart. With ends even, thread both ends of jute string through a natural 1/2-in. bead. Then add a green 1/2-in. bead, a red 1/2-in. bead and another natural 1/2-in. bead.

Tie ends of jute string in a knot close to last bead. Then tie jute string in a bow to the loop of an arm of one snowman. Repeat, adding jute string and beads to remaining hearts and joining them to the arms of other snowmen. In the same way, add jute string and beads to the arms at each end of garland.

Tie a felt strip around neck of each snowman as shown in photo.

Roll out your frosty garland during December!

Her Simple Sheep Ornament Is Woolly Fun for All Ages!

A SHEAR delight—that's what young and old alike will think when they give this fuzzy trimmer a try! "Ewe" will enjoy making it, too, since it's so quick and easy, assures Doris Schmidt of Cincinnati, Ohio.

"I based the design on the twin lambs we had at the time," she tells. "It's been a favorite ornament among family and friends ever since."

Materials Needed:
Pattern on this page
Tracing paper and pencil
Compass
Two 4-inch squares of white fake fur
4-inch square of white poster board
3-inch square of gray felt
Two 3mm black beads
Two cinnamon sticks
Sprig of miniature artificial pine bough
One 10mm gold jingle bell
One 1/2-inch-diameter red ribbon rose
1/4-inch-wide satin ribbon—6 inches
  of green and 9 inches of red
Low-temperature glue gun and glue stick
Scissors

Finished Size: Wooly sheep measures about 3 inches across x 5 inches tall with hanger.

Directions:
Trace head pattern onto tracing paper and cut out pattern.

Trace around pattern onto gray felt and cut out head.

Use compass to draw a 3-in. circle onto tracing paper. Cut two circles from fake fur and one circle from poster board.

Referring to photo for placement, glue head onto fur side of one fake fur circle. Glue jingle bell below head and beads to head for eyes.

Cut a 3-in. length of red ribbon for hanger. Glue ends together to make a loop. Glue ends to wrong side of fake fur circle above head.

Work with remaining ribbons as one and tie ribbons into a small bow.

Glue pine bough and a tuft of fake fur to top of head. Glue bow over tuft of fake fur and ribbon rose to center of bow.

Glue cinnamon stick legs to wrong side of same circle, leaving about 1 in. of

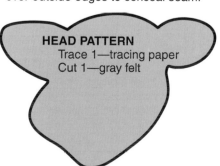

each extending beyond edge of circle.

Glue poster board circle centered onto wrong side of remaining circle of fake fur. Glue circles together with edges matching and fur sides out. Work fake fur over outside edges to conceal seam.

HEAD PATTERN
Trace 1—tracing paper
Cut 1—gray felt

Simple Santa's Ingrained with Noel Charm

YOU don't have to go out on a limb to bring the holidays into your home. Just add this dashing gent from the North Pole—he'll figure in festiveness fast!

California crafter Janna Britton cut out and embellished basic wood shapes to form her Father Christmas.

"The simple fabric sack will hold almost anything," she notes from her home in Firebaugh. "You can fill it with greens like I did or toss in candies, little wrapped packages or potpourri."

Materials Needed:
Pattern on this page
Tracing paper and pencil
17-inch length of 1 x 6 pine lumber (actual size about 3/4 inch x 5-1/2 inches)
Scroll saw
Sandpaper and tack cloth
15-inch-long x 1/2-inch-wide piece of off-white fake fur
White curly doll hair
6-inch x 11-inch piece of red and green plaid fabric
Matching all-purpose thread
4 inches of 1/4-inch-wide elastic
Paper plate or palette
Paper towels
Water basin
Acrylic craft paints—black, flesh, ivory and red
Small flat paintbrush
Low-temperature glue gun and glue sticks
Artificial evergreens
Standard sewing supplies

Finished Size: Santa measures 5-1/4 inches wide x 3-1/2 inches deep x 11-1/4 inches tall.

Directions:
Mark tracing paper with a 1-in. grid and draw pattern onto tracing paper as shown. Or use copy machine to enlarge pattern 200%. Cut out pattern.

Use scroll saw to cut a 5-1/4-in.-long x 3-1/2-in.-wide piece from one end of 1 x 6 lumber for base.

Place Santa pattern onto remaining wood piece with grain lines matching and trace around outside edges. Cut out on traced lines with scroll saw.

Sand shapes to smooth and wipe with tack cloth to remove sanding dust.

Turn Santa pattern over and rub flat side of pencil lead over face section of pattern to darken. Place pattern right side up over Santa cutout with edges matching. Trace over face section to transfer pattern onto wood.

Place small amount of paint onto paper plate or palette as needed. Keep water basin handy to thin paint as directed and to clean brushes.

Thin red paint with a bit of water and basecoat Santa with thinned paint, leav-

ing face unpainted. Let dry.

Paint the circle for the face with flesh. Let dry. Dip the handle of the brush into

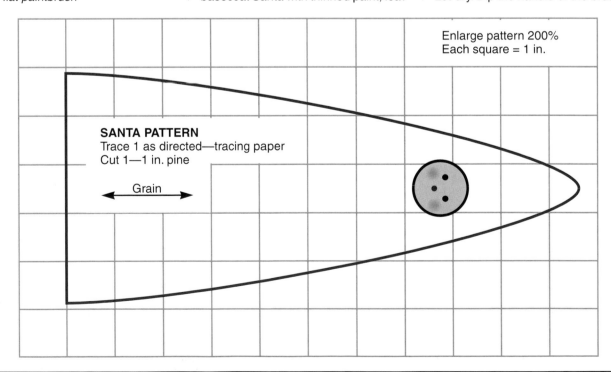

SANTA PATTERN
Trace 1 as directed—tracing paper
Cut 1—1 in. pine

← Grain →

Enlarge pattern 200%
Each square = 1 in.

Fig. 1 Stitching bottom of sack

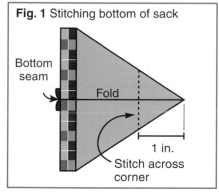

Bottom seam

Fold

1 in.

Stitch across corner

the paint and dab on two small black dots for the eyes and one small red dot for the nose. Let dry.

Dip paintbrush into red and wipe excess paint onto paper towel until no brush streaks show. Then paint Santa's cheeks with a circular motion. Let dry.

Paint wooden base ivory. Let dry.

Center and glue Santa along length of base 1/2 in. from back edge as shown in photo.

Wrap fake fur strip around bottom of Santa with seam in front. Glue to secure and trim excess.

Glue remaining fake fur around top of Santa's face for hair.

Take a few 2-in.-long strands of curly doll hair and wrap center with a short piece of thread for mustache.

Glue remaining curly doll hair to Santa's face for beard. Then glue mustache below nose. Trim beard in a "U" shape as shown in photo.

Fold fabric for sack in half crosswise to make a 5-1/2-in. x 6-in. rectangle. Sew sides opposite fold with a 1/2-in. seam.

Fold one raw edge 1/4 in. to wrong side and press. Fold again 1/2 in. to wrong side to form a casing for elastic and press. Sew close to first fold, leaving a small opening to insert elastic.

Center seam and sew across end opposite casing with a 1/2-in. seam.

To make a flat bottom on sack, match bottom seam of sack with side fold and sew across corner 1 in. from end. See Fig. 1. Match bottom seam with other side fold and stitch as before. Turn sack right side out.

Pin safety pin to one end of elastic and thread elastic through casing. Draw up elastic and overlap ends, leaving a 3-in. opening in top of sack. Hand-sew ends of elastic together.

Glue sack to front of Santa and to base as shown in photo.

Fill sack with artificial evergreens. Add Santa to your holiday decor! 🔔

These Critter Trims Are the Cat's Meow!

PURRFECTLY adorable and quick to raise, these fabric kitties from Chris Pfefferkorn of New Braunfels, Texas will happily brighten a tree or top a package with Christmas cheer.

"You can also add a loop of fabric to the back of each cat's body and use them as napkin rings any time of year," suggests Chris.

"If you don't want to trim the edges with pinking shears," she adds, "brush white glue that's been diluted with water on the edges to seal them."

Materials Needed (for one):
Pattern on this page
Tracing paper and pencil
Two 4-1/2-inch x 5-1/2-inch pieces of red and white check fabric or green, red and white plaid fabric
Matching or contrasting all-purpose thread
Six-strand embroidery floss—green for collar and red for hanger (optional)
Embroidery needle
Polyester stuffing
8mm gold jingle bell for check fabric cat (optional)
8 inches of 3/8-inch-wide red satin ribbon for plaid fabric cat (optional)

Pinking shears
Standard sewing supplies

Finished Size: Each fabric cat is about 4-1/4 inches high x 3-1/2 inches across.

Directions:
Trace pattern onto tracing paper.

Pin two pieces of matching fabrics with wrong sides together and edges matching. Place the pattern on top of the fabric with grain lines matching.

With matching or contrasting thread, sew over traced lines of pattern with straight stitch, leaving opening where indicated on pattern. Remove pattern.

Stuff cat lightly. Sew opening closed as before.

Using pinking shears, trim around outside edges a scant 1/4 in. outside stitching.

Thread jingle bell onto green floss and tie floss around neck for collar. Or tie ribbon in a small bow and hand-sew bow to cat's neck as shown in photo.

Cut a 1/2-in. x 4-in. strip of matching fabric. Fold in half lengthwise, folding long raw edges in. Sew folds together along length of strip. Fold strip in half crosswise. Hand-sew ends to the back of cat's head for hanging loop. Or stitch a loop of embroidery floss to back of head for hanger.

Enjoy your kitty! 🔔

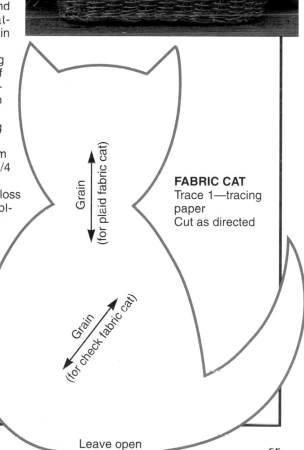

Grain
(for plaid fabric cat)

Grain
(for check fabric cat)

FABRIC CAT
Trace 1—tracing paper
Cut as directed

Leave open

Cute Yo-Yo Accessories Add Festive Touch to Any Outfit

THE TURNAROUND time on these fashionable earrings and matching hair clip is pretty quick—but the effects are long-lasting!

"It's simply a matter of making yo-yos with fabric scraps and adding ribbon," confirms Pat Ford of Arlington, Texas, who designed the duo. "They bring lots of compliments, too.

"I originally intended my accessories to resemble apples," she adds. "But the colors I chose are so merry, they work well for the holidays."

Materials Needed (for all):
Tracing paper and pencil
Compass
5-inch x 12-inch piece of red and white plaid fabric
5-inch square of red and white print fabric
Matching thread and hand-sewing needle
3/4 yard of 1/4-inch-wide green satin ribbon
1 yard of 1-inch-wide green and white striped grosgrain ribbon
3-inch square of poster board
Two 10mm flat-pad earring posts with clutches or two flat-pad clip earring backs

3-inch barrette (available in the jewelry findings section of most craft stores)
Low-temperature glue gun and glue stick
Scissors

Finished Size: Each earring is about 1-1/2 inches across. The barrette is about 6 inches long x 5 inches high.

Directions:
EARRINGS: Use compass to draw a 1-in. circle and a 3-1/4-in. circle onto tracing paper. Cut out circles for patterns.

From red and white plaid, cut two 3-1/4-in. circles.

From 3-in. square of poster board, cut two 1-in. circles.

Thread hand-sewing needle with matching thread and knot ends together. Turn edge of one red and white plaid fabric circle 1/4 in. to wrong side. Stitch close to folded edge of circle with running stitch. See Fig. 1.

Pull thread gently to draw up fabric circle into a puff and fasten off. Flatten puff with your fingers and center opening as shown in Fig. 2. Repeat for other earring.

Cut two 8-in.-long pieces of green satin ribbon. Tie each in a small bow. Glue bow onto edge of back of yo-yo, concealing knot and bending loops toward edge. Trim ribbon ends at an angle.

Glue poster board circle centered on back of yo-yo. Center and glue an earring back to back of each earring.

BARRETTE: Use compass to draw a 4-1/4-in. circle onto tracing paper. Cut out circle for pattern.

From red and white print, cut one 4-1/4-in. circle.

Construct yo-yo as directed above.

Cut a 12-in.-long piece of green satin ribbon. Tie ribbon into a 2-in.-long bow. Glue bow onto edge of back of yo-yo, concealing knot and bending loops toward edge. Trim ribbon ends at an angle.

Form green and white striped ribbon into a bow as shown in Fig. 3. Hand-tack center of bow to hold. Trim ends at an angle to desired length.

Glue bow to front of barrette and completed yo-yo to center of bow.

Fig. 1 Making yo-yo

Fig. 2 Finished yo-yo

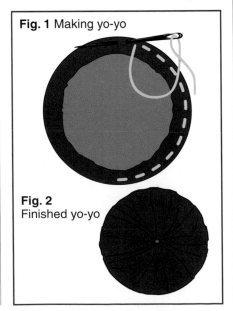

Fig. 3 Making bow

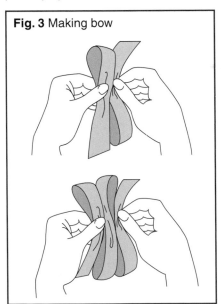

Pretty Paper Wreath Rolls Out Lacy Look for Boughs

YOU'LL put a new spin on the family fir when you brighten its branches with this delicate adornment. The lacy wreath is sure to sprout smiles when folks catch a glimpse of it!

Don't worry if it looks complicated. "The quilling isn't difficult," assures Jody Ondrus of Maple Heights, Ohio. "Once you start with this technique, you won't want to stop."

Materials Needed:
1/8-inch-wide quilling paper or construction paper cut into 1/8-inch-wide strips—green, red and white
Corsage pin, round toothpick or quilling tool for rolling paper
Straight pin or toothpick
Waxed paper
White (tacky) glue
Ruler
Nylon thread
Scissors

Finished Size: Poinsettia wreath measures about 3-1/2 inches across x 4-3/4 inches high.

Directions:
BASIC QUILLING INSTRUCTIONS:
To roll paper coils, tear off a strip of 1/8-in.-wide quilling or construction paper to the length specified in the instructions.

Place end of paper into slotted quilling tool and roll to the end. If using a toothpick or corsage pin as a tool to roll paper, moisten one end of paper slightly and press it onto the pin or toothpick. Roll paper onto tool.

Slide tool out and glue end in place or allow coil to open to desired size, then glue end in place. Strive for uniformity between like shapes.

Prepare shapes as directed, noting that lengths given represent lengths of paper strips to tear, not lengths or widths of rolled shapes.

When gluing shapes together, place them on waxed paper and use a toothpick to place a drop of glue wherever the shapes touch.

Refer to Fig. 1 for quilling shapes used.
POINSETTIAS (make four): Tear six 2-in. lengths of red paper. Form each into a curved petal about 3/8 in. long. Glue petals together to form top layer of poinsettia as shown in photo.

Tear six 4-in. lengths of red paper. Form each into a curved petal about 1/2 in. long. Glue petals together to form bottom layer of poinsettia as shown in photo. Let dry.

Tear ten 1/2-in. lengths of yellow paper. Cut each strip in half lengthwise. Form each strip into open coils for centers of flowers. Let dry.

Glue top layer of poinsettia centered onto bottom layer with petals alternating as shown in photo. Let dry.

Place a small amount of glue onto center of each poinsettia and gently press five yellow open coils into glue. Let dry.
BABY'S BREATH: Tear sixteen 1-in. lengths of white paper. Cut each strip from corner to corner and form each into a ball shape.

For stems, tear two 3-in. lengths of white paper. Spread a thin layer of glue on one side of each strip. Fold the strips in half crosswise and press halves together. When dry, cut each strip in half lengthwise.

Apply glue to each side of stem and press eight ball shapes onto each stem. Let dry.
WREATH: Glue two 24-in.-long strips of green paper together end to end to make a strip about 48 in. long. Make three more strips in the same way.

Make spirals out of each of the strips.

Working with three spirals as one, gently shape spirals into a 3-1/2-in. circle for wreath. Wrap remaining spiral loosely around wreath, alternating from inside to outside of circle. Twist ends together to secure.

BOW: Tear eight 2-in. lengths of red paper. Glue ends of each together to make a loop. Glue four loops to each side at bottom of wreath with glued ends meeting.

Tear two 1-1/2-in. and two 3-in. lengths of red paper. Form each into a spiral. Glue spirals over ends of loops.

ASSEMBLY: Referring to photo for placement, glue four poinsettias around wreath. Insert stems of baby's breath into coils of wreath between poinsettias and glue to secure.

FINISHING: Thread a 6-in. piece of nylon thread into top of wreath and knot ends together for hanger.

Hang on the tree and watch it wrap up smiles fast!

Fig. 1 Quilling Shapes

Spiral:
Wrap paper down around length of tool in a spiral. Continue to wrap paper, making a long tendril or curl.

Ball Shape:
Cut paper strip from corner to corner. Roll wide end toward narrow end. Glue end before removing from tool.

Open Coil:
Roll a tight coil without gluing end. Slip it off tool and let coil expand to desired size.

Curved Petal:
Roll a tight coil without gluing end. Slip off the tool and let it expand to desired size. Glue end. When dry, pinch opposite sides of coil, curving one end up and one end down.

Nifty Knit Stocking's Piled High with Snowy Delights!

CHOCK-FULL of frosty fun, this bright stocking's sure to whip up a flurry of smiles come Christmastime. What's more, knitter Louise Purpura of Valparaiso, Indiana sized it right so plenty of goodies can be packed inside.

Want to personalize it a bit more? Add a name and date to the stocking instead of "Let It Snow".

Materials Needed:
Chart on next page
Worsted-weight yarn—4 ounces each of red and white
Worsted-weight sparkle yarn (yarn with a metallic thread)—1.75 ounces each of green, white and variegated green, red and white
Knitting needles—pair of straight and set (four needles) of double-pointed in size 8 (5mm) or size needed to obtain correct gauge
Stitch marker

Stitch holders—two small and one large
Size C/2 (2.75mm) crochet hook
Tapestry needle
3/4 yard of 44-inch-wide 100% cotton or cotton-blend fabric for lining
Matching all-purpose thread
1/2-inch red pom-pom
Small jingle bell (optional)
Standard sewing supplies

Finished Size:
Stocking is about 22 inches long.

Gauge: When working in St st, 5 sts = 1 inch.

KNITTING REMINDERS:
Changing colors: To avoid holes when changing colors, always pick up the new color of yarn from beneath the dropped yarn.

Working in rounds: Place sts evenly on 3 dp needles. Place a marker at the beginning of the round, moving the marker with each round worked. Being careful not to twist sts, join the last st to the first st by pulling up yarn firmly and making first st with fourth needle.

Stockinette stitch: St st
　Row 1 (RS): Knit across row.
　Row 2 (WS): Purl across row.
　Repeat Rows 1 and 2.
K 2, p 2 ribbing:
　Every Row: K 2, p 2 across row.

Directions:
With straight knitting needles and red, cast on 60 sts.
　Rows 1-10: Work in k 2, p 2 ribbing: 60 sts.
　Rows 11-12: With variegated sparkle yarn, k both rows.
　Rows 13-14: With red, work in St st.
　Rows 15-26: With white and green, work "Let It Snow" section of chart in St st, starting at the bottom of the chart. Read chart from right to left for a knit row and from left to right for a purl row.
　Rows 27-28: With red, work in St st.
　Rows 29-30: With variegated sparkle yarn, k both rows.
　Rows 31-34: With red, work in St st.
　Rows: 35-66: With colors indicated on the chart, work the snowman section in St st the same as for the "Let It Snow" section, except purl green sts for the hatband in Rows 38 and 39 and decrease 1 st at each end of every tenth

row until you have 54 sts.
　Rows 67-70: With red, work in St st: 54 sts.
　Rows 71-72: With variegated sparkle yarn, k both rows.
　Rows 73-80: With red, work in St st: 54 sts.
　Top of foot: Row 81: K 41, sl last 13 sts on small holder for heel.
　Row 82: P 28, sl last 13 sts on second small holder for heel.
　Rows 83-94: Work in St st on 28 sts. Slip sts onto large holder.
　HEEL: Rows 1-11: Slip 13 sts of each side of heel from holders onto one dp needle so that the ends of the rows are at middle of needle. With RS facing and red yarn, work in St st on 26 sts for 11 rows.
　Turning heel: Row 12: P 15, p 2 tog, p 1, turn.
　Heel Row 13: Sl 1, k 5, sl 1, k 1, psso, k 1, turn.
　Heel Row 14: Sl 1, p 6, p 2 tog, p 1, turn.
　Heel Row 15: Sl 1, k 7, sl 1, k 1, psso, k 1, turn.
　Heel Row 16: Sl 1, p 8, p 2 tog, p 1, turn.
　Heel Row 17: Sl 1, k 9, sl 1, k 1, psso, k 1, turn.
　Heel Row 18: Sl 1, p 10, p 2 tog, p 1, turn.
　Heel Row 19: Sl 1, k 11, sl 1, k 1, psso, k 1, turn.
　Heel Row 20: Sl 1, p 12, p 2 tog, p 1, turn.
　Heel Row 21: Sl 1, k 13, sl 1, k 1, psso, k 1, turn. Break off yarn.
　Heel Row 22: Join red at top right-hand side of heel: Pick up and k across 12 sts along side of heel, k 16 sts of heel, pick up and k 12 sts along remaining side of heel: 40 sts.
　Heel Row 23: P across row.
　Heel Row 24: K 1, sl 1, k 1, psso, k to last 3 sts, k 2 tog, k 1.
　Repeat Rows 23 and 24 until 26 sts remain, ending with a k row: 26 sts.
　FOOT: Round 1: (See knitting reminders for working in rounds.) Sl last 13 sts just worked from straight needle onto first dp needle. On second needle, k across 28 sts on holder; on third needle, k remaining 13 sts. Center of heel is now at beginning of each round: 54 sts.
　Rounds 2-15: K each round.
　Toe Shaping: Round 16: Change to white, on first needle, k 13; on second needle, k 1, sl 1, k 1, psso, k to last 3 sts, k 2 tog, k 1. On third needle, k 13.
　Round 17: Knit.
　Round 18: On first needle, k to last 3 sts, k 2 tog, k 1; on second needle, k 1, sl 1, k 1, psso, k to last 3 sts, k 2 tog, k 1. On third needle, k 1, sl 1, k 1, psso, k

to end of round.

Repeat Rounds 17 and 18 until 8 sts remain. Break off yarn and run end through all sts. Draw up yarn tightly and fasten off on inside of stocking.

FINISHING: Thread tapestry needle with white yarn and randomly stitch snowflakes on front of stocking around snowman. See Fig. 1 for stitch illustration.

Referring to chart and photo for position, stitch red nose and mouth and black eyes. Then add a long black stitch for each arm. See Figs. 2 and 3 for stitch illustrations.

Use hand-sewing needle and thread to stitch pom-pom to front of snowman.

Use tapestry needle and matching yarn to sew back seam and sides of instep of stocking.

Hanging Loop: Using any color yarn, ch 10. Fasten off, leaving an 8-in. yarn end. Fold chain in half and use yarn end to stitch both ends of chain to back seam at top edge of stocking.

Lining: Fold lining fabric with right sides together. Lay knitted stocking on top of fabric. Cut around stocking 1/2 in. from all edges. With right sides together, machine-stitch 1/2 in. from edges, leaving top edge open.

Fold 2 in. of top edge to wrong side for hem. Trim hem to 1/2 in. from fold. With lining wrong side out, put lining inside stocking, positioning the top edge of lining 1-1/2 in. from the top edge of the stocking.

Add jingle bell between layers if desired, working it down to tip of toe.

Use matching thread to hand-stitch the top edge of the lining to the inside of the stocking.

Pack with little presents and hang up with care! 🔔

ABBREVIATIONS

ch	chain
dec	decrease
dp	double-pointed
k	knit
p	purl
psso	pass the slipped stitch over
RS	right side
sl	slip
st(s)	stitch(es)
tog	together
WS	wrong side

Fig. 1 Stitching snowflakes and eyes

Fig. 2 Stitching nose

Fig. 3 Stitching mouth

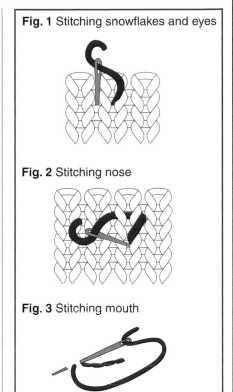

CHART

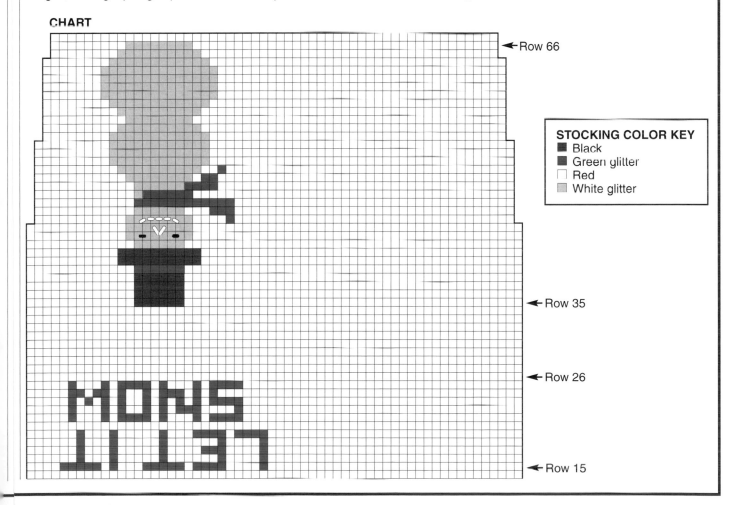

← Row 66

← Row 35

← Row 26

← Row 15

STOCKING COLOR KEY
- ■ Black
- ■ Green glitter
- □ Red
- ▨ White glitter

Kids Will Tune in to These Trims!

RINGING with fun, these bright bells from Mary Cosgrove of Rockville, Connecticut are sure to elicit peals of laughter when youngsters tackle them.

"All that's needed to make the trims are cleaned-out plastic containers, acrylic paint and a few other easy supplies," Mary notes. "The red bell takes a bit more practice due to the crackle finish I added."

Materials Needed (for both):
*Two clean, dry plastic yogurt
    containers or 8-ounce Styrofoam
    cups*
Paper plate or palette
*Acrylic craft paints—gold metallic and
    red (Mary used Delta Ceramcoat
    Fire Red and Gleams Metallic 14K
    Gold paints)*
*Crackle finish (Mary used Delta
    Crackle Medium)*
Small flat paintbrush
*Three red pipe cleaners (chenille
    stems)*
Six 1/2-inch jingle bells
Two 2- or 4-hole buttons
White (tacky) glue

Craft scissors or wire cutters
Nylon thread

Finished Size: Each bell measures about 3 inches wide x 4-1/2 inches tall.

Directions:
PAINTING: Place small amounts of paints on paper plate or palette as needed.

Apply additional coats of paint as needed for complete coverage, allowing drying time between coats of paint.

Paint entire surface (inside and out) of each plastic container or cup metallic gold. Let dry.

Paint buttons and jingle bells metallic gold. Let dry.

Apply crackle finish to outside of one container only following manufacturer's directions. Then apply red paint to outside of same container. Let dry.

Cut one pipe cleaner in half. Fold one length in half. Thread ends of pipe cleaner through a button from back to front. Then fold ends back to center, making two loops for bow as shown in photo.

Twist ends close to button to secure the bow. Repeat, using the other half of pipe cleaner and the other button.

Invert each container and glue flat side of one button centered onto bottom of each container.

Thread three bells onto center of one remaining pipe cleaner. Gently fold pipe cleaner in half and twist ends together, making a 4-in.-long loop. Repeat, using remaining pipe cleaner and bells.

Glue ends of pipe cleaners to inside bottoms of containers, allowing bells to extend about 1 in. below container.

Tie a loop of nylon thread to bow for hanger.

Hang on the tree and enjoy!

Scrappy Evergreen Shirt's a Snap to Make

THIS pretty top has a practical side that's fascinating. To attach the balsam embellishment, you simply snap it in place!

"I came up with this kind of design so I could toss the shirt in the wash and not worry that the trim might come off," Carol Howell of Seminole, Oklahoma says.

"By adding snaps to each point on the tree, I can put the accent on and take it off without any trouble."

Materials Needed:
Patterns on next page
Tracing paper and pencil
Purchased white sweatshirt
*10-inch x 12-inch piece of heavy-weight
    iron-on interfacing*
*Fabric scraps—10-inch x 12-inch piece
    of dark green solid for tree and 2-1/2-
    inch square of brown solid for tree
    trunk (Carol used suedecloth fabrics)*
*2-1/2 yards of 1-inch-wide pre-gathered
    green Cluny lace*
Matching all-purpose thread

2 yards of 1/8-inch-wide yellow ribbon
*10 wooden Christmas charms or nov-
    elty buttons*
*One 1-1/2-inch gold metallic
    embroidered star*
13 small snaps
Large-eye hand-sewing needle
Standard sewing supplies

Finished Size: Tree measures about 8-1/2 inches across x 12 inches high.

Directions:
Trace patterns onto folded tracing paper. Cut out shapes and open for complete patterns. Trace around shapes onto iron-on interfacing.

Fuse shapes centered onto wrong side of fabrics as directed on patterns. Cut out the tree and the trunk on outside traced lines.

Place tree shape fabric side up on a flat surface. Center trunk along bottom edge of tree so edges are meeting but not overlapping. Stitch around entire trunk with brown thread and a medium satin stitch, catching bottom edge of tree when stitching across top of trunk.

Referring to Fig. 1, sew lace to tree in overlapping layers as follows: Using matching thread, sew a row of lace onto tree so lace extends a bit beyond bottom edge of tree and pre-gathered edge is about 3/4 in. from bottom edge of tree. Trim ends even with sides of tree. Add another row of lace in same way, making sure bottom edge of new row covers top edge of previous row.

Continue to add rows of lace in this way until entire tree shape is covered with lace.

Stitch around sides of tree with green thread and a medium satin stitch, stitching through all layers and catching ends of lace in stitching. Stitch across bottom of tree without catching lace trim in stitching. Do not stitch around trunk.

Hand-sew star to top of tree.

Cut ribbon into ten 7-in. lengths. Thread large-eye sewing needle with ribbon and thread a charm on ribbon. Stitch ribbon through opening in lace. Remove needle and tie ribbon in a bow. Trim ends at an angle to desired length.

Hand-sew one side of each snap to top of tree, ends of branches and bottom corners of trunk.

Place the completed tree on the front of the sweatshirt. Mark position of snaps and sew other side of snaps to marked points on front of sweatshirt.

Snap the tree onto your sweatshirt—and don your snazzy top! 🔔

Fig. 1
Lace Placement

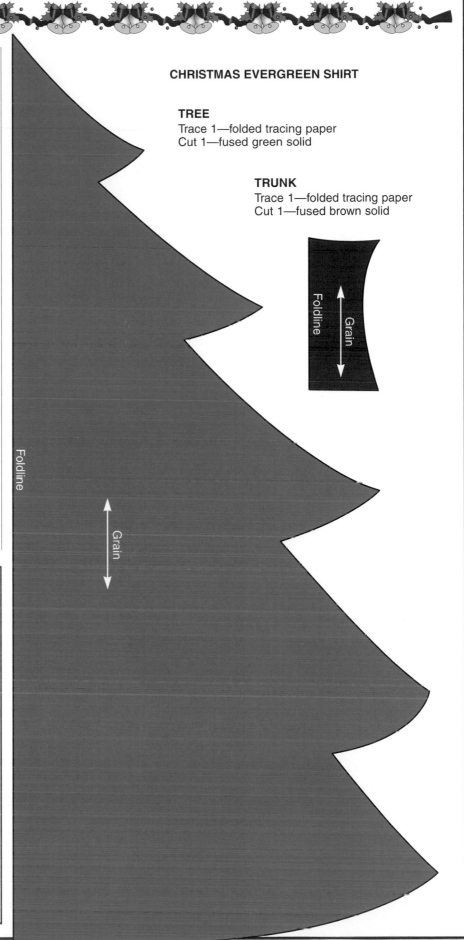

CHRISTMAS EVERGREEN SHIRT

TREE
Trace 1—folded tracing paper
Cut 1—fused green solid

TRUNK
Trace 1—folded tracing paper
Cut 1—fused brown solid

Reindeer Quilt's Aglow for Christmas

WANT to brighten your decor during December? Consider rounding up this endearing accent from Della Byers of Rosamond, California—it'll highlight any setting just right!

Don't confine the design, though— you can expand Della's wall hanging into a lap or bed quilt by adding more appliqued blocks. Or make just one and turn it into a pillow top.

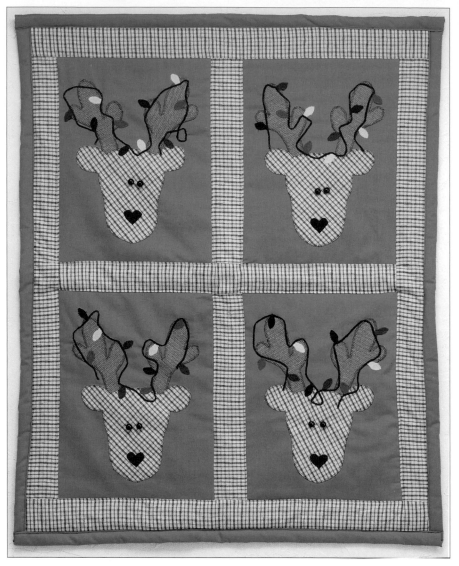

Materials Needed:

Patterns on next page
Tracing paper and pencil
44-inch-wide 100% cotton or cotton-blend fabrics—2-1/4 yards of green solid for blocks and backing; 1 yard of tan, green and red plaid for appliques and sashings; 1/4 yard of brown check for antlers; and scraps of blue solid, purple solid, red solid and yellow solid for lights and nose appliques
Matching all-purpose thread
1 yard of paper-backed fusible web
Tear-away stabilizer or typing paper
Quilter's marking pen or pencil
Rotary cutter and mat (optional)
Eight 1/2-inch black ball buttons for eyes
4 yards of 1/8-inch-wide red satin ribbon
35-inch x 45-inch piece of lightweight quilt batting
Standard sewing supplies
30 inches of 1/4-inch wooden dowel (optional)

Finished Size: Reindeer quilt is 33-1/2 inches wide x 43-1/2 inches long.

Directions:

Pre-wash fabrics, washing each color separately. If the water from any fabric is discolored, wash again until rinse water runs clear. Dry and press all fabrics.

Do all piecing with accurate 1/4-in. seams and right sides of fabrics together. Press seams toward darker fabrics when possible.

CUTTING: Cut quilt blocks and sashing strips using rotary cutter and quilter's ruler or mark fabrics using ruler and marker of choice and cut with scissors.

From green solid, cut a 35-in. x 45-in. piece for backing and four 11-1/2-in. x 16-1/2-in. pieces for blocks.

From tan, green and red plaid, cut two 3-1/2-in. x 16-1/2-in. strips and one 3-1/2-in. x 25-1/2-in. strip for sashing. Also, cut two 3-1/2-in. x 35-1/2-in. strips and two 3-1/2-in. x 31-1/2-in. strips for borders.

APPLIQUES: Trace patterns onto tracing paper as directed on patterns.

Trace around patterns onto paper-back fusible web, leaving 1/2 in. between shapes. Cut shapes apart.

Following manufacturer's directions, fuse shapes to wrong side of fabrics as directed on patterns. Cut out shapes on traced lines.

Remove paper backing from heads and antlers and fuse them onto the right side of green blocks as shown in the photo. Then fuse a nose onto each head. Fuse 10 lightbulbs of four different colors randomly around antlers in each block.

Position tear-away stabilizer or typing paper on wrong side of the green blocks behind the designs. Using matching thread and a small machine blanket stitch or medium satin stitch, applique around each antler and then around each head. In the same way, stitch around each nose and all lightbulbs.

Cut ribbon into four 36-in.-long pieces. Pin a length of ribbon from lightbulb to lightbulb on each block as shown in photo. Use matching thread and a zigzag stitch to hold ribbon in place.

Remove tear-away stabilizer or typing paper. Pull all threads to wrong side and secure.

Hand-sew buttons to heads for eyes as shown in photo.

ASSEMBLY: Do all piecing with accurate 1/4-in. seams, right sides of fabrics together and edges matching. Press seams toward darker fabrics. Lay out all pieces as shown in photo.

Sew a 3-1/2-in. x 16-1/2-in. sashing between blocks in each row. Sew a 3-1/2-

in. x 25-1/2-in. sashing between rows.

Sew a 3-1/2-in. x 35-1/2-in. border strip to each side of pieced top. Then sew remaining border strips to top and bottom edges.

QUILTING: Place backing wrong side up on a flat surface and smooth out wrinkles. Place batting centered over backing and smooth out. Center pieced top over batting, right side up, and smooth out.

Hand-baste through all three layers, stitching from center to corners, then horizontally and vertically every 4 in. until layers are securely held together.

Using thread to match sashings in the needle and thread to match backing in the bobbin, stitch 1/4 in. outside seams around each block. Machine- or hand-baste around outer edges of pieced top.

Trim away excess batting and backing, cutting 1-1/4 in. from edge of pieced top.

BINDING: Fold and press 1/2 in. along one side edge of backing to wrong side. Fold batting and backing to front of pieced top, encasing raw edges and leaving a 1-in.-wide border of backing fabric showing. Machine-sew fold of backing to front of quilt. Repeat on other side edge and then do the same on top and bottom edges.

HANGING SLEEVE (optional): From a scrap of backing fabric, cut two 3-in. x 15-in. rectangles. Stitch a 1/4-in. hem to the wrong side of each short edge of each hanging sleeve.

Fold each long edge 1/2 in. to wrong side. Pin hanging sleeves to backing along top edge of quilt, spacing them about 1/2 in. apart at the center top. Hand-stitch folds of hanging sleeves to backing only.

Insert dowel in hanging sleeves to hang. Accent a wall with this merry reindeer quilt!

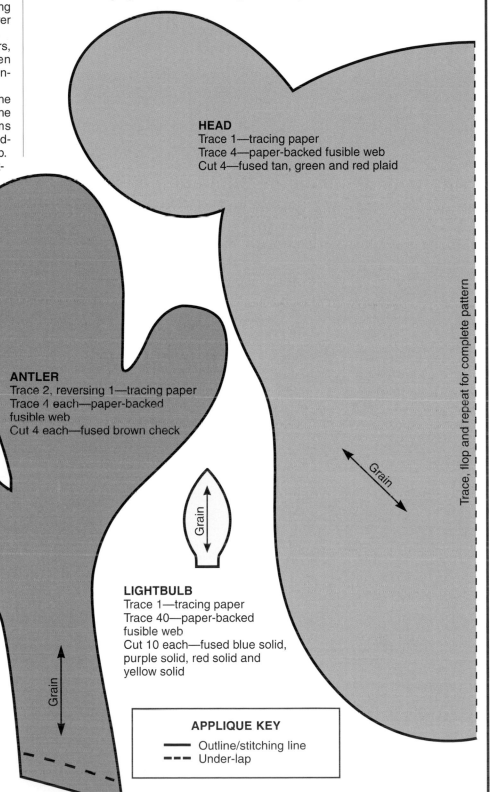

HEAD
Trace 1—tracing paper
Trace 4—paper-backed fusible web
Cut 4—fused tan, green and red plaid

ANTLER
Trace 2, reversing 1—tracing paper
Trace 4 each—paper-backed fusible web
Cut 4 each—fused brown check

LIGHTBULB
Trace 1—tracing paper
Trace 40—paper-backed fusible web
Cut 10 each—fused blue solid, purple solid, red solid and yellow solid

NOSE
Trace 1—tracing paper
Trace 4—paper-backed fusible web
Cut 4—fused red solid

Trace, flop and repeat for complete pattern

Grain

APPLIQUE KEY	
——	Outline/stitching line
- - -	Under-lap

Wooden Accents Are Cut Out for Noel Decor

PINING for new ways to trim your tree? These pretty ornaments from Carla Bauer will add a festive air to boughs in no time.

Carla, who hails from Pagosa Springs, Colorado, sawed simple holiday shapes, then painted them in rustic tones sure to suit any color scheme.

Not only can the accents brighten branches, they'll also look lovely hanging in a window, from a garland, on a wreath or wherever you prefer.

Materials Needed (for both):
Tracing paper and pencil
Scroll or band saw
Drill with 3/32-inch bit
Sandpaper and tack cloth
Paper plate or palette
Paper towel or soft cloth
Paintbrushes—small flat, fine liner and old scruffy brush or toothbrush
Black permanent fine-line marker
2-ply jute string
Clear acrylic spray sealer
Glue gun and glue sticks
Scissors

Materials Needed (for tree):
Tree pattern on this page
4-inch square of 1/4-inch-thick basswood
1/8-inch-thick purchased wood cutouts—one 1/2-inch-high star, five 1/2-inch-high hearts and one 3/4-inch-high heart

Acrylic craft paints—bright red, dark blue, dark red, green, light blue, light green, ivory, white and yellow
6 inches of 1/8-inch-wide red satin ribbon

Materials Needed (for stocking):
Stocking pattern on next page
5 inches of 1 x 4 pine (actual dimensions are 3/4 inch x 3-1/2 inches)
Acrylic craft paints—black, brick red, blue, flesh, green, ivory, mauve and golden brown
6 inches of green six-strand embroidery floss or heavy thread
Blue fabric—three 6-inch-long x 1/8-inch-wide strips and one 6-inch-long x 1/4-inch-wide strip

Finished Size: Tree trim is 3-1/2 inches high x 3-7/8 inches across. Stocking is 3 inches across x 4-1/4 inches long. Measurements do not include the hangers.

Directions:
TREE: Trace pattern onto tracing paper. Trace around the pattern onto 4-in. square of basswood and cut out tree with scroll or band saw.

Drill hole through top of tree where indicated on pattern. Sand lightly and wipe with tack cloth.

Using flat brush, paint entire tree green. Paint large heart ivory and star yellow. Paint the five small hearts light blue, dark blue, light green, dark red and bright red. When pieces are dry, lightly sand each to expose wood on edges to give a worn look.

Place painted tree on a protected surface. Dip scruffy brush or toothbrush into thinned white paint. Hold brush a few inches from tree and draw the handle of a paintbrush or your thumb across the bristles. Repeat until desired look is achieved. Let dry.

Glue hearts and star onto tree as shown in photo. When dry, spray entire tree with sealer.

Using marker, write "LOVE", "JOY", "PEACE", "HOPE" and "FAITH" on the five small hearts as shown on pattern. In the same way, write "NOEL" on the large heart and add outside stitching lines to large heart and star.

Thread a 6-in. piece of jute string through drilled hole at top of tree and tie ends in a small bow for hanger. Tie ribbon into a small bow and glue bow to center of jute bow.

STOCKING: Trace pattern onto tracing paper and cut out. Trace pattern onto 1 x 4 pine and cut out using scroll or band saw. Drill holes at each X where indicated on the pattern. Sand lightly and wipe with a tack cloth.

TREE PATTERN
Trace 1—tracing paper
Cut 1—1/4-in. basswood

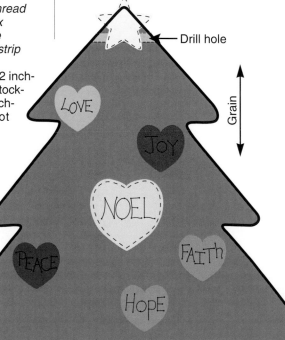

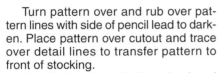

Turn pattern over and rub over pattern lines with side of pencil lead to darken. Place pattern over cutout and trace over detail lines to transfer pattern to front of stocking.

Use flat brush to paint front, back and sides of body of stocking brick red and heel and toe of stocking green. Let dry.

Referring to pattern, paint bear golden brown. Paint rag doll's face and hand flesh and sleeve blue. Let dry.

Paint cheeks on bear and rag doll mauve. Let dry.

Paint heart and bear's hand, muzzle and inside of ears ivory. Use liner to paint cross-hatch pattern on heel and toe ivory. Dip liner into ivory and dab several tiny dots randomly on body of stocking. Let dry.

Place stocking on a protected surface. Dip scruffy brush or toothbrush into thinned black paint. Hold brush a few inches from piece and draw handle of paint brush or your thumb across bristles. Repeat until the desired look is achieved. Let dry.

Lightly sand stocking to expose wood on edges to give a worn look.

Spray with sealer. Let dry.

STOCKING

Trace 1—tracing paper
Cut 1—1 x 4 pine

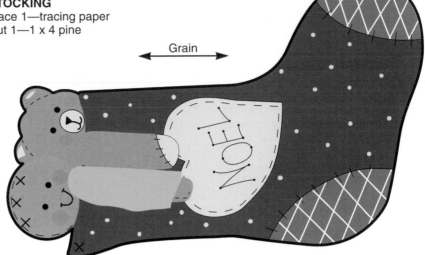

Grain

Use black marker to add stitching, lettering and all remaining details as shown on pattern.

Tie green floss or thread into a tiny bow and glue bow to top of bear's head where shown in photo.

Thread an 1/8-in.-wide fabric scrap through each drilled hole on rag doll and tie ends in an overhand knot. Trim ends close to knot.

Cut a piece of jute string to desired length for hanger. Thread hanger through drilled hole at top of stocking and tie ends in a bow. Tie remaining blue fabric strip into a small bow and glue bow over ends of hanger. 🔔

Bear Cherub Heralds Holidays

PERCH this beaming beast on a branch and watch it usher in the spirit of the season…along with a host of happy grins!

Aside from brightening the tree, this merry bear angel from Bette Veinot of Bridgewater, Nova Scotia can affix an added dash of fashion to any outfit. Simply glue on a pin back behind the ribbon wings…and it'll become a brooch.

Materials Needed:
Pom-poms—one 1-1/4-inch tan for head and three 1/2-inch tan for ears and muzzle
Three 5mm black beads for eyes and nose
6 inches of strawberry blonde curly doll hair
7-3/4 inches of 1-1/2-inch-wide burgundy velvet ribbon
6 inches of 3/8-inch-wide burgundy, green and gold metallic striped ribbon for bow
4-1/4 inches of green silk mini garland for halo*
Eight 3mm gold metallic beads
3-1/2-inch-round Battenburg lace doily
3 inches of gold metallic cord for hanger

Glue gun and glue stick
Scissors

* If you can't find a mini garland, Bette suggests using a 4-inch length of pre-strung 3mm gold beads.

Finished Size: Angel bear ornament is 3-3/4 inches wide x 2-1/2 inches tall.

Directions:
Glue a 1/2-in. pom-pom to one side of 1-1/4-in. pom-pom for muzzle. Glue two remaining 1/2-in. pom-poms above muzzle for ears where shown in photo.

Glue two beads above muzzle for eyes and one to tip of muzzle for nose.

Glue doll hair to top of head between ears, extending a bit onto the forehead.

Wrap ends of garland together to make a circle for halo. Glue seven gold beads around halo and glue halo to angel bear's head as shown in photo. Let dry.

Overlap narrow ends of velvet ribbon slightly. Center ends in back and glue to hold, making a flat bow 3-3/4 in. across. Use scissors to round top and bottom edges slightly to make a bow shape.

Cut doily in half, following design of doily. Glue doily centered along velvet ribbon with straight edge of doily about 1/4 in. from top edge of velvet ribbon.

Glue head of angel bear centered along straight edge of doily.

Tie striped ribbon into a small bow. Glue a gold bead to center of bow. Glue bow to lace below angel bear's head.

Trim the tree with your angelic critter creation! 🔔

Country Cozy Suits Christmas to a 'T'!

DRINKING IN the joys of the season couldn't be more fun with this delightful teapot cover! With its whimsical merry mouse motif cross-stitched on front, the cozy encourages smiles even as it keeps fresh-brewed beverages nice and toasty.

Designer Darlene Polachic of Saskatoon, Saskatchewan points out that the needlework can be framed by itself or added to a pillow top.

"Those mice are fun wherever they pop up," she adds with a laugh.

Materials Needed:
Chart on next page
8-inch x 10-inch piece of antique white 16-count Aida cloth
DMC six-strand embroidery floss in colors listed on color key
One red quilted place mat
One package of 1/2-inch-wide double-fold bias tape to match place mat
1 yard of 1/2-inch-wide white lace trim
Matching all-purpose thread
Standard sewing supplies

Finished Size: Tea cozy measures about 13 inches wide x 10 inches high. The design area is 77 stitches wide x 71 stitches high.

Directions:
Zigzag or overcast edges of Aida cloth to prevent fraying. Fold Aida cloth in half lengthwise and then in half crosswise to determine the center and mark this point.

To find center of chart, draw lines across chart connecting arrows. Begin stitching at this point so design will be centered.

Working with 18-in. lengths of six-strand floss, separate strands and use two strands for cross-stitching and one strand for backstitching. See Fig. 1 for stitch illustrations.

Each square on chart equals one stitch worked over a set of fabric threads. Use colors indicated on color key to complete cross-stitching, then backstitching.

Do not knot floss on back of work. Instead, leave a short tail of floss on

back of work and hold it in place while working the first few stitches over it. To end a strand, run needle under a few neighboring stitches in back before cutting floss close to work.

When stitching is completed, and only if necessary, wash gently in lukewarm water. Press right side down on terry towel to dry.

ASSEMBLY: Fold place mat in half crosswise. Cut along fold, making a front and back piece for tea cozy.

Sew bias tape along curved edge of one half of place mat. Starting and stopping with a fold to the wrong side, sew bias tape along the straight edge, encasing the raw edge. Repeat on the other half of place mat.

Trim stitched Aida cloth, leaving piece 7-3/4 in. wide x 6-3/4 in. high with design centered.

Center completed design right side up on right side of one half of place mat with bottom edge of Aida cloth parallel to straight edge of place mat. Sew around outside edges of Aida cloth with matching thread and a zigzag stitch.

TEA COZY CHART

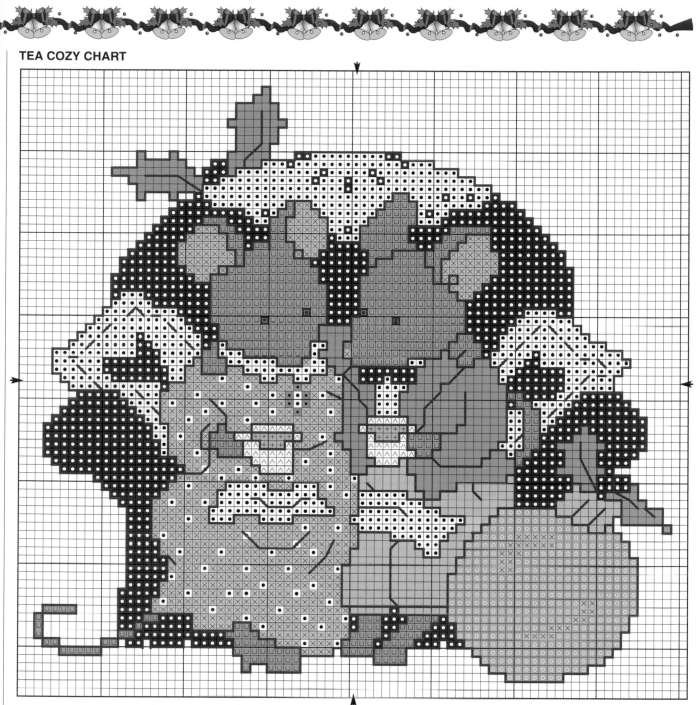

Sew straight edge of lace trim to edges of Aida cloth, covering previous zigzag or overcast stitching.

Pin halves of place mats together with right sides out and edges matching to make tea cozy.

Cut a 5-in.-long piece of bias tape. Fold tape in half with ends matching to form a loop. Slip ends of loop between front and back pieces at top of tea cozy as shown in photo.

Sew front and back of cozy together with matching thread, stitching just inside edge of bias tape. Sew along the curved edge only, catching the ends of loop in stitching and leaving the straight edge open.

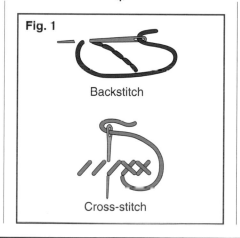

Fig. 1

Backstitch

Cross-stitch

CROSS-STITCHED TEA COZY
COLOR KEY   **DMC**

- ⊡ White ....
- ▣ Black 310
- ▨ Pearl Gray 415
- ⊞ Very Light Brown 435
- ▨ Dark Beige Gray 642
- ▨ Christmas Green Bright 700
- △ Very Light Topaz 727
- ◻ Very Dark Coral 817
- ▨ Very Light Golden Olive 834
- ⊠ Ultra Very Light Dusty Rose ..963
- ▪ Black Brown 3371

BACKSTITCHING
- — Black Brown 3371

Sprucing Up Any Setting Is What Pine Finery Does Best

TREE TABLE TOPPER PATTERNS
A
Trace 1—folded tracing paper
Cut 4 each—green print and white-on-white print

BRANCH OUT by adding this pretty topper to your holiday decor, and you'll wind up with a table that's rooted in true balsam beauty!

Claire Kelley from Cincinnati, Ohio "sowed" the simple appliqued design using a basic green and white color scheme, although she notes you can add in other tones to match your decor if you like.

Materials Needed:
Patterns on this page and next page
Tracing paper and pencil
44-inch-wide 100% cotton or cotton-blend fabrics—2/3 yard of green print for piecing, appliques and backing and 1/4 yard of white-on-white print for piecing
Green all-purpose thread
6-inch x 18-inch piece of paper-backed fusible web
Tear-away stabilizer or typing paper
20-inch square of lightweight quilt batting
Standard sewing supplies

Finished Size: Table topper measures about 19 inches across.

Directions:
Pre-wash all fabrics, washing colors separately. If the water from any fabric is discolored, wash again until rinse water runs clear. Machine-dry and press all fabrics.

Trace patterns on this page and top of next page onto folded tracing paper. Cut out each piece and open for complete patterns.

CUTTING: From green print fabric, cut a 20-in. square for backing and a 7-in. x 19-in. piece for appliques. Then cut four of A and one of B as directed on pattern.

From white-on-white print, cut four of A as directed on the pattern.

APPLIQUE: Center the fusible web on wrong side of 7-in. x 19-in. piece of green print. Fuse in place following manufacturer's directions.

Place tree shape on paper side of fused fabric with grain lines matching. Trace around shape. Repeat three more times. Cut out shapes on traced lines.

Remove paper backing from trees. Fuse a tree to right side of each white-on-white print A piece, leaving a 1/2-in. margin on each side at bottom of trees.

Place tear-away stabilizer or typing paper on wrong side behind appliques. Stitch around trees with matching thread and a medium satin stitch.

Remove tear-away stabilizer or typing paper. Pull threads to back side and secure.

PIECING: Lay out alternating green print and white-on-white print pieces on flat surface with right sides up and long edges of pieces touching.

With right sides together and long edges matching, sew pieces with a 1/4-in. seam in planned order. Press seams toward darker fabric.

Place green print B piece with right side up on right side at center of pieced top. Sew around circle with matching thread and a medium satin stitch. Pull threads to back side and secure.

ASSEMBLY: Place square of batting on a flat surface and smooth out wrinkles. Center backing fabric right side up on top of batting. Place pieced top wrong side up on top of batting. Pin through all layers to secure.

Sew around pieced top, stitching 1/4 in. from outside edge of pieced top and leaving an opening for turning. Remove pins. Trim excess batting and backing, leaving a 1/4-in. seam allowance. Clip corners.

Turn right side out through opening so batting is on the inside. Turn raw edges of opening in and hand-sew opening closed.

Topstitch around outside with green thread, stitching 1/4 in. from seam.

Grain

Foldline

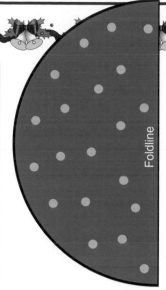

B
Trace 1—folded tracing paper
Cut 1—green print

Foldline

Grain

TREE
Trace 1—folded tracing paper
Cut 4—fused green print

Foldline

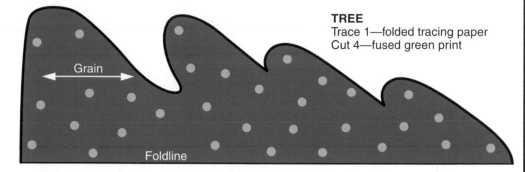

Materials Needed (for poinsettia gift tag):
Miniature red poinsettia flower
Gold glitter
6 inches of 1/4-inch-wide red satin ribbon

Finished Size: Each gift tag is about 3-1/2 inches long x 2 inches high.

Directions:
CANDY GIFT TAG: Cut red or green ribbon in half. Tie red ribbons around twisted ends of wrapped green candy or green ribbons around twisted ends of wrapped red candy. Trim ends of ribbons at an angle.

Glue wrapped candy to upper left corner of paper or card stock. Let dry.

HOLLY GIFT TAG: Glue holly leaves to the left side of paper or card stock. Let dry.

Glue rosebud centered over holly leaves. Let dry.

Cut ribbon into three equal lengths. Glue ends of each length together to form a loop. Glue loops around base of rosebud. Let dry.

POINSETTIA GIFT TAG: Remove stem from flower. Apply a thin band of glue to edge of flower. Use finger to spread a thin layer of glue over right side of leaf. Sprinkle glitter onto wet glue. Remove excess glitter and let dry.

Glue leaf and flower to left side of paper or card stock. Let dry.

Fold ribbon in half and glue ends to upper left corner of paper behind flower. Let dry.

FINISHING: Use marker to write "To" and "From" on front of gift tags.

Apply double-stick tape to back of each gift tag. Attach tags to gifts. Give to family members and friends. ♧

Gift Tags Tie Up Fun Fast

PERSONALIZING presents won't take but a minute when you give Paula Del Favero's designs a try. The crafty mom from Deerfield Beach, Florida cut stiff paper into rectangles, then attached fitting festive trims such as ribbons and wrapped candy.

"The tags are so easy. In fact, the craft's perfect for youngsters to tackle," she suggests.

Materials Needed (for each):
3-1/2-inch x 2-inch piece of white heavy paper or card stock
White (tacky) glue
Black fine-line permanent marker
Double-stick tape
Scissors

Materials Needed (for candy gift tag):
Wrapped green or red peppermint candy
6 inches of green or red 1/8-inch-wide satin ribbon

Materials Needed (for holly gift tag):
Three artificial green and white holly leaves
One 1/2-inch red rosebud
12 inches of 1/8-inch-wide red satin ribbon

Plastic Canvas Boxes Hold Heaps of Cheer

OVERFLOWING with Christmas spirit, these clever containers are perfectly matched for stylish storage, whether you nestle napkins inside, fill them with candy or pour in potpourri.

"The boxes are so easy to make from plastic canvas," reveals Sharon Murphy of Mississauga, Ontario. "Even a beginner will make swift work of this Yuletide duo."

Materials Needed (for both):
Charts on next page
Two 10-1/2-inch x 13-1/2-inch sheets of clear 7-count plastic canvas
Glue gun and glue stick
Size 16 tapestry needle
Scissors

Materials Needed (for Santa box):
4-ply worsted-weight or plastic canvas yarn—1/3 yard of black, 19 yards of green, 1/3 yard of light pink, 1 yard of red and 15 yards of white
One 1/2-inch white tinsel pom-pom

Materials Needed (for snowman box):
4-ply worsted-weight or plastic canvas yarn—3 yards of black, 1/3 yard of bright pink, 17 yards of green, 1/3 yard of orange, 1 yard of red and 13 yards of white
Two small artificial holly leaves with red berries

Finished Size: Each box is about 4-1/2 inches square x 1-7/8 inches high.

Directions:
FOR EACH BOX: Being sure to count the bars and not the holes, cut plastic canvas according to the charts. Also

cut one 29-bar x 29-bar piece for bottom of each box.

STITCHING: Working with 18- to 20-in. lengths of yarn, follow charts on next page and individual instructions that follow to stitch each piece. See Fig. 1 for stitch illustrations.

Do not knot the yarn on back of work. Instead, leave a 1-in. tail on the back and catch it in the first few stitches. To end a yarn, run yarn on back of canvas under completed stitches of the same color and clip close to work.

Lid top: Santa: Following Santa chart, use Continental stitch and white to stitch border and green to stitch background. Then fill in Santa's hat with red and his beard with white. Add light pink

face and black eyes.

Stitch Santa's nose with red cross-stitches.

Fill in mustache with white slanted and reverse slanted Gobelin stitches. Then overcast edges and backstitch center of mustache.

Glue pom-pom to Santa's hat and mustache below his nose.

Lid top: Snowman: Following snowman chart, use Continental stitch and white for border and green for background. Then fill in hat with black and red and face with white. Add orange carrot nose and black eyes.

Fill in snowman's cheeks with bright pink Scotch stitches.

Backstitch mouth with black. Glue

Fig. 1

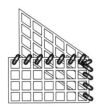

Backstitch

Scotch stitch

Cross-stitch

Slanted Gobelin

Whipstitch/Overcast

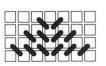

Leaf stitch

Continental stitch

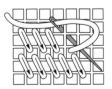

Reverse Slanted Gobelin

PLASTIC CANVAS BOXES

SANTA LID CHART
31 x 31 bars
Cut 1—plastic canvas

SNOWMAN LID CHART
31 x 31 bars
Cut 1—plastic canvas

BOX SIDE CHART
29 x 12 bars
Cut 4 for each box—plastic canvas

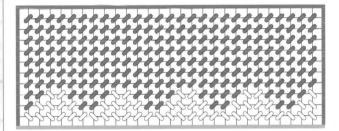

LID SIDE CHART
31 x 6 bars
Cut 4 for each box—plastic canvas

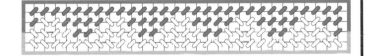

SANTA'S MUSTACHE
4 x 10 bars
Cut 1—plastic canvas

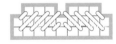

holly to hat as shown in photo.

Lid side (make four for each box): Fill in each side with green Continental and white leaf stitches, leaving outside edges unstitched.

Box side (make four for each box): Fill in each side with green Continental and white leaf stitches, leaving outside edges unstitched.

ASSEMBLY: Referring to photo, assemble each gift box as follows: Whipstitch the bottom edges of four stitched box sides to edges of unstitched bottom piece, making sure that the right sides face outward.

Whipstitch a Santa or snowman lid

top to the top edges of the four lid sides with green yarn, making sure that the right sides face the same direction. Then whipstitch the corners together with matching yarn.

Place completed lid on gift box. 🔔

• Plastic canvas projects made with acrylic yarn may be hand washed. Carefully swish the completed piece through warm water with a mild detergent without rubbing or scrubbing. Blot excess moisture onto a towel and allow item to air dry away from heat.

PLASTIC CANVAS GIFT BOXES COLOR AND STITCH KEY
CONTINENTAL STITCH
- Black
- Green
- Light pink
- Orange
- Red
- White

CROSS-STITCH
- Red

SCOTCH STITCH
- Bright pink

SLANTED GOBELIN
- White

REVERSE SLANTED GOBELIN
- White

LEAF STITCH
- White

BACKSTITCH
- Black

WHIPSTITCH/OVERCAST
- Green
- White

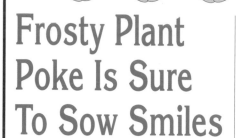

Frosty Plant Poke Is Sure To Sow Smiles

BLOOMING with Christmas cheer is this gourdgeous guy from Betty Souther of Dos Palos, California.

"I used a small gourd to form his head," says the crafty lady. "Orange oven-bake clay makes up his carrot nose, and a red sock hat suits my snowman up just right."

What's best about the festive snowman is the fact that he'll never melt. "He'll warm up a potted poinsettia or other houseplant for years," Betty beams.

Materials Needed:
3-inch round gourd or papier-mache ball
9 inches of 1/8-inch wooden dowel
Drill with 1/8-inch bit
Orange oven-bake polymer clay (Betty used Sculpey III)
White acrylic craft paint and small paintbrush
Powdered cosmetic blush
Cotton swab
Black permanent fine-line marker
Man's red sock
Matching all-purpose thread
Toothpick
Glue gun and glue stick
Hand-sewing needle
3/4-inch white pom-pom
Scissors

Finished Size: Plant poke is about 3 inches across x 10 inches high.

Directions:
Drill hole in gourd opposite stem. Insert dowel into hole, leaving about 6 in. of dowel exposed. Glue to hold.

Form clay into a small cone shape about 5/8 in. tall for nose. Use toothpick to make small indentations around cone to resemble carrot. Bake as directed by manufacturer.

Paint gourd white. Let dry.

Cut a 4-in.-wide band of ribbing from top of sock for hat. Turn band inside out. Thread hand needle with red thread. Stitch around cut edge of sock to gather. Turn right side out so stitching is on inside. Sew pom-pom to top of hat.

Draw face on gourd with marker as shown in photo. Let dry.

Use cotton swab to apply powdered blush to cheeks. Dip toothpick into white paint and dab a tiny dot on each eye.

Glue carrot onto gourd for nose.

Place hat on top of gourd. Fold back edge for cuff of hat and glue as needed.

Stick your snowman among some indoor greenery! 🔔

Deck Your Halls with These Fantastic Wall Treatments!

IT'S A BREEZE to assemble these accessories from Ellena Hand of Huntsville, Alabama. "I love the old-fashioned feeling they create," she remarks.

"Plus, they're terrific for using up all my scraps of fabric, ribbons and odds and ends I find in my sewing box."

Materials Needed (for each):
Patterns on next page
Tracing paper and pencil
12-inch x 7-inch piece of lightweight cardboard
12-inch x 7-inch piece of green felt
2-3/4-inch-wide craft ribbon—6-inch lengths of seven different green, red and white background Christmas prints
6 inches of gold metallic thread for hanger (optional)
White (tacky) glue
Scissors

Materials Needed (for patchwork fan):
1 yard of coordinating cording or tube ribbon
24 inches of 1/8-inch-wide red satin ribbon
Two 1/2-inch silver jingle bells

Materials Needed (for angle-top fan):
1 yard of 1/2-inch-wide red satin picot ribbon
Three 1/2-inch white frosted bells or other trims

Finished Size: Each fan is about 6 inches tall x 11 inches across.

Directions:
Trace patterns onto tracing paper as directed on patterns. Cut out patterns.

PATCHWORK FAN: Trace around background pattern onto lightweight cardboard. Cut out cardboard background.

Place section pattern on right side of one piece of ribbon with grain lines matching. Cut out shape. Repeat, making a total of seven.

Apply a thin coat of glue to right side of lightweight cardboard.

Starting at left edge, glue a piece of ribbon to cardboard with left straight edge of ribbon even with left straight edge of cardboard. Smooth out wrinkles.

Add another piece of ribbon, overlapping straight edge of new ribbon over previous ribbon about 1/8 in. Continue to add remaining ribbons in same way, alternating background colors of ribbons. Let dry.

Trim excess ribbon even with outside edge of cardboard background.

Apply glue to back of fan. Center felt over back of fan. Smooth out wrinkles. Let dry.

Trim excess felt even with outside edge of cardboard background.

Finishing: Tie a small knot 1/2 in. from one end of 1/8-in.-wide red ribbon. Glue knot to top left edge of right side of fan. Tie another knot even with next seam. Glue knot to right side of fan as shown in photo. Continue in same way to opposite edge of fan.

Trim excess and glue ends of ribbon to back of fan.

Tie cording or tube ribbon in a bow as shown in photo. Glue bow to center bottom of fan. Trim ends to desired length. Glue jingle bells to ends.

Glue ends of metallic thread centered onto top back of fan for hanger if desired.

ANGLE-TOP FAN: Follow instructions for patchwork fan. Complete the patchwork ribbon front and apply the felt to the back of fan.

To make angled top, make a 3/8-in.-long cut where each patchwork section joins. Cut straight across top of each section, cutting from top of far right corner of each section straight across to bottom of each 3/8-in. cut as shown on patchwork section pattern.

Finishing: Tie picot ribbon into a multi-loop bow as shown in photo. Glue bow to center bottom of fan.

Glue bells onto bow.

Glue ends of metallic thread centered onto top back of fan for hanger if desired.

DECORATIVE FAN PATTERNS

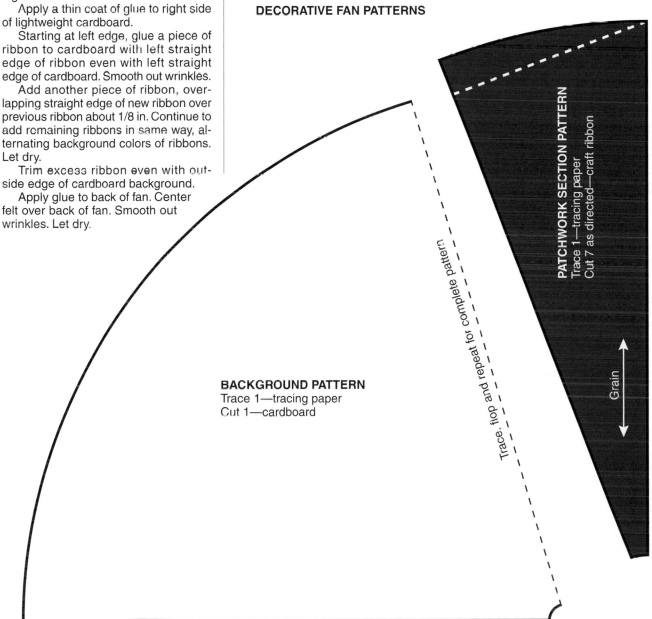

BACKGROUND PATTERN
Trace 1—tracing paper
Cut 1—cardboard

Trace, flop and repeat for complete pattern

PATCHWORK SECTION PATTERN
Trace 1—tracing paper
Cut 7 as directed—craft ribbon

Grain

Lively Appliqued Tree Skirt Spices Up Any Setting Nicely

ROUND OUT your December decor by draping the base of a balsam with this tasteful wrapper from Pamela Houk of Sherwood, Arkansas. It'll spruce up the room in seconds!

Not only are the sweet motifs fanciful, they're also fancy-free—thanks to no-sew appliqueing and simple fabric painting. Even the ribbon trim's a cinch to add with fusible web.

Materials Needed:

Patterns on next page
Tracing paper and pencil
44-inch-wide 100% cotton or cotton-blend fabrics—1-1/3 yards of unbleached muslin for tree skirt; 1/4 yard each of tan and brown check for gingerbread men and red and white stripe for candy cane appliques; 1/8 yard each or scraps of green print for bow tie and holly and red pin-dot for heart appliques
5-1/2 yards of 3/8-inch-wide green satin picot ribbon
Dimensional fabric paints—black, brown, green, white and red
1 yard of paper-backed fusible web
6-1/2 yards of 3/8-inch-wide fusible web tape
Pencil

Quilter's marking pen or pencil
Measuring tape
Scissors
Iron and ironing surface

Finished Size:

Tree skirt measures 44 inches across.

Directions:

Pre-wash and dry all fabrics without fabric softeners or stain resistors, washing colors separately. Press all fabrics.

CUTTING: Cut a 44-in. square of muslin. Fold square in half lengthwise, then fold in half crosswise. Measure and mark an arc with quilter's marking pen or pencil 2-1/2 in. from point of folds as shown in Fig. 1.

In same way, draw an arc 22 in. from point of folds. Cut along both marked lines and open for a 44-in. circle with a 5-in. center circle.

Draw a line from center circle to outside edge. Cut along line to make opening for tree skirt. Press 1/2 in. to wrong side along both sides of opening for hem. Following manufacturer's directions, fuse hem in place with 3/8-in.-wide fusible web.

Cut a piece of picot ribbon equal to the distance around the outside of the circle plus 1 in. Cut a same-size piece of 3/8-in.-wide fusible web. Starting and

ending with a 1/2-in. fold to wrong side, fuse ribbon to right side of outside edge of tree skirt as shown in photo.

In same way, center and fuse remaining ribbon around edge of center circle of tree skirt. Leave ends of ribbons to use for ties.

APPLIQUES: Trace gingerbread man onto tracing paper as directed on pattern. Also trace candy cane pattern onto tracing paper and cut out.

Trace around gingerbread man five times onto paper side of fusible web. Trace around candy cane four times onto paper side of fusible web.

Reverse candy cane pattern and trace around shape four more times onto paper side of fusible web. Cut shapes apart.

Trace heart, bow tie and holly patterns onto paper side of fusible web as directed on patterns, leaving 1/2 in. between shapes. Cut shapes apart.

Fuse shapes onto wrong side of fabrics as directed on patterns following manufacturer's directions. Cut out shapes on traced lines.

Referring to photo for placement, center and fuse a gingerbread man onto right side of tree skirt with bottom of shape about 2-1/2 in. from outer edge.

Fuse remaining gingerbread shapes around tree skirt with tips of arms about 11 in. apart. Then fuse a bow tie and heart onto each.

Fuse candy canes between gingerbread men as shown in photo. Then add holly to each set of candy canes.

Fuse remaining holly to tree skirt as shown in photo.

DIMENSIONAL PAINTING: Place tree skirt right side up on a flat protected surface.

Outline each gingerbread man with brown paint. Let dry.

Add white zigzag trim and white buttons to each gingerbread man where shown on pattern. Outline each candy cane with white. Let dry.

Use black to add eyes and a mouth to each gingerbread man.

Outline holly and each bow tie with green. Then add a vein to center of each leaf. Let dry.

Add a small red dot to each gingerbread man for a nose and a small red dot to center of each bow tie. Outline each heart with red and add small dots on each side of white zigzag trim. Then add three red dots to centers of holly for holly berries. Let dry.

Highlight each holly berry with a tiny dot of white. Let dry.

Wrap up your tree sweetly! 🔔

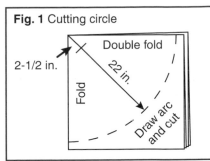

Fig. 1 Cutting circle

Double fold

2-1/2 in.

Fold

22 in.

Draw arc and cut

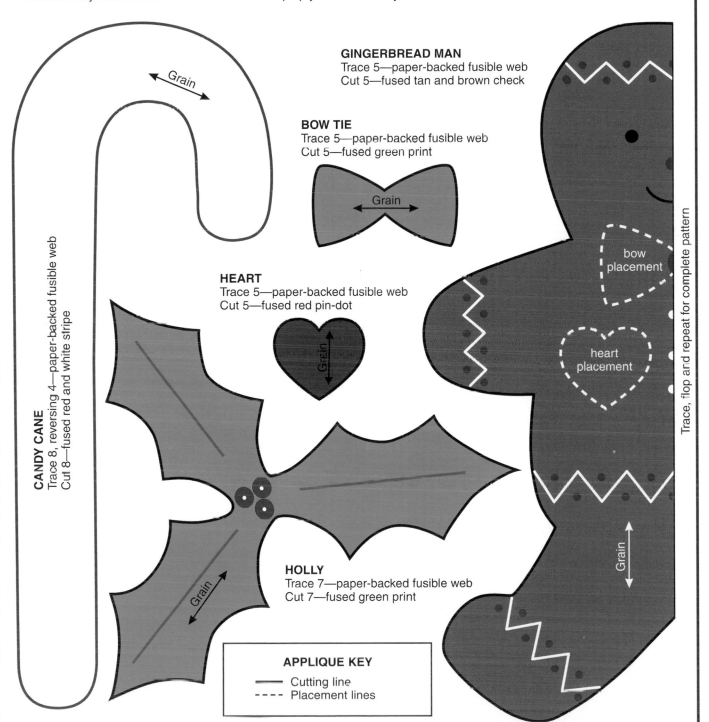

GINGERBREAD MAN
Trace 5—paper-backed fusible web
Cut 5—fused tan and brown check

BOW TIE
Trace 5—paper-backed fusible web
Cut 5—fused green print

Grain

HEART
Trace 5—paper-backed fusible web
Cut 5—fused red pin-dot

Grain

CANDY CANE
Trace 8, reversing 4—paper-backed fusible web
Cut 8—fused red and white stripe

Grain

HOLLY
Trace 7—paper-backed fusible web
Cut 7—fused green print

Grain

bow placement

heart placement

Grain

Trace, flop and repeat for complete pattern

APPLIQUE KEY
—— Cutting line
- - - Placement lines

Merry Making's in the Bag With These Scrappy Sachets

THE lively aromatic packets from Helen Rafson of Louisville, Kentucky are simply scent-sational!

"Filled with potpourri, they make nice hostess gifts or stocking stuffers," she says.

"I used a no-sew technique to attach the appliques," Helen adds. "That keeps the sacks fast, which is important at this busy time of year."

Materials Needed (for each):
Patterns on this page
Pencil
Pinking shears
14-inch-long piece of 3-ply jute string
Standard sewing supplies
Sachet or potpourri

Materials Needed (for tree bag):
100% cotton or cotton-blend fabrics—two 4-1/8-inch x 6-7/8-inch pieces of muslin and scraps of brown, gold and green prints for appliques
Off-white all-purpose thread
5-inch square of paper-backed fusible web

Materials Needed (for reindeer bag):
100% cotton or cotton-blend fabrics—one 7-1/2-inch x 6-3/4-inch piece of green print and scraps of tan print and light brown solid
All-purpose thread to match green print
5-inch square of paper-backed fusible web
6 inches of 1/4-inch-wide red satin ribbon
Black fine-line permanent marker
7mm red pom-pom
White (tacky) glue

Finished Size: The tree sachet bag measures approximately 4 inches across x 6-3/4 inches tall. The reindeer sachet bag measures approximately 3-1/2 inches across x 6-1/2 inches tall.

Directions:
TREE BAG: Trace individual tree pattern pieces onto the paper side of fusible web, leaving 1/2 in. between shapes. Cut shapes apart.

Pin muslin pieces with wrong sides together and edges matching. Sew pieces together with matching thread and a 3/8-in. seam, stitching along long edges and across one end. Leave other end open.

Use pinking shears to trim seam allowance to 1/4 in. from stitching and to trim a scant 1/4 in. from top (open) end of bag. Press.

Fuse shapes onto wrong side of fabrics as indicated on patterns following manufacturer's directions.

Cut out shapes on traced lines. Remove paper backing.

Place star, tree and trunk shapes fabric side up on right side of muslin bag, positioning them as shown in photo. Fuse shapes in place.

REINDEER BAG: Trace individual reindeer pattern pieces onto paper side of fusible web, including under-laps and leaving 1/2 in. between shapes. Cut shapes apart.

Fold green print piece in half crosswise with right sides together and edges matching to make a 3-3/4-in. x 6-3/4-in. piece.

Sew raw edges together with matching thread and a 1/4-in. seam, stitching opposite fold and across one end. Leave other end open. Clip corners.

Turn right side out through opening.

SACHET BAG PATTERNS
Trace 1 each—paper side of fusible web
Cut 1 each—fabric indicated on pattern

TREE PATTERNS

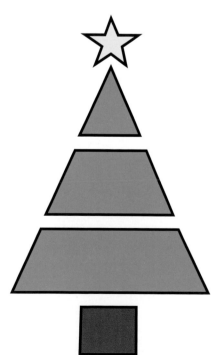

REINDEER PATTERNS

APPLIQUE KEY
—— Outline
- - - Under-lap
— Inside design line

Press. Use pinking shears to trim a scant 1/4 in. from the top (open) end of the bag.

Place reindeer head and antlers fabric side up on right side of green print bag, positioning them as shown in photo. Fuse shapes in place.

Use the permanent marker to add small dots for eyes, eyebrows, smiling mouth and lines on ears as shown on reindeer pattern.

Tie red ribbon in a small bow. Glue bow to reindeer below mouth.

Glue pom-pom nose above mouth where shown on pattern.

FINISHING: Fill bags with sachet or potpourri. Wrap a length of jute string tightly around top of each sack and tie ends in a small bow. Trim ends to desired length.

Use as a fragrant party favor or give to a friend!

Jewelry Is a Jolly Fit for Christmas!

SOMETIMES all an outfit needs is a simple necklace or pin to give it a happy holiday feeling. That's why Verlyn King of Tremonton, Utah created these nifty Noel pieces.

The Santa pin is groomed for fastening on for festive occasions, while the brightly colored necklace bears a sure sign of glad tidings. Plus, both are a cinch to paint and put together!

Materials Needed (for Santa pin):
3-inch-long x 5/8-inch-wide x 1/4-inch-thick miniature wooden canoe paddle or oar
3/8-inch-high x 1-1/4-inch-long x 1/8-inch-thick wooden mustache or angel wing
1/4-inch domed wooden furniture plug
Paper plate or palette
Acrylic craft paints—black, flesh, red and white
Clear acrylic sealer
Paintbrushes—small flat and liner
Two 2mm glue-on wiggle eyes
3/8-inch white pom-pom
1-1/4-inch pin back
Glue gun and glue stick

Materials Needed (for necklace):
Three 3/4-inch natural wooden blocks with pre-drilled centers
Paper plate or palette
Acrylic craft paints—green, red and white
Paintbrushes—small flat, small round and spatter brush or old toothbrush
Newspaper
Clear acrylic spray sealer
Pony beads—two green, two red and four white
Tapestry needle

28 inches of 1/8-inch-wide red satin ribbon
Scissors

Finished Size: Santa pin measures 1-1/4 inches across x 3-1/4 inches long. Necklace is about 26 inches long.

Directions:
SANTA PIN: Glue mustache or angel wing to paddle about 3/4 in. from round end of paddle as shown in photo. Glue wooden furniture plug above center of mustache for nose. Glue pin back to back of paddle.

Place small amounts of paints on paper plate or palette as needed. Paint pieces as directed, extending paints onto sides of each piece.

Apply a second coat as needed for complete coverage, allowing drying time between each coat.

Use flat brush and flesh to paint nose and face as shown in photo. Let dry.

Use flat brush and white to paint beard, mustache and fur trim on hat. Let dry.

Use flat brush and red to paint hat. With nearly dry brush and a circular motion, add red to cheeks and nose. Let dry.

Use liner to add white highlight to nose.

Use liner and black to outline mustache, beard, fur trim and hat as shown in photo. Let dry.

Apply sealer to entire pin. Let dry.

Glue wiggle eyes above nose and pom-pom to top of hat.

NECKLACE: Use flat brush to paint all sides of two blocks red and all sides of one block green. Let dry.

Place painted blocks on newspaper to protect surfaces around and underneath them.

Mix about a teaspoon of white paint with an equal amount of water. Dip spatter brush or old toothbrush into thinned paint. Hold bristles about 8 in. from blocks and pull another brush handle or your finger across bristles. Repeat, spattering all sides of each block. Let dry.

Use round brush and white to write "HO" on one undrilled side of each block. Let dry. Repeat on remaining three undrilled sides of each block.

Spray blocks with sealer. Let dry.

Thread tapestry needle with ribbon. Slide a red, white and green pony bead onto ribbon. Then add a red block and a white bead. Add a green block and white pony bead. Finally, add a red block and a green, white and red bead.

Center beads and blocks along length of ribbon.

With ends of ribbon even, tie ends in a knot. Trim ends of ribbon at an angle.

Dress up outfit with these accents!

Sweater Sports Festive Style

BUTTON UP Yule cheer with this warm and winning kid-size knit sweater from designer Janet Mysse of Ingomar, Montana.

"Bright red and white yarns give this garment its seasonal appeal, but you can mix and match any colors you want," Janet describes, adding that this cardigan was designed with more experienced knitters in mind.

Materials Needed:
Knitting patterns on this page
Worsted-weight yarn—6(7,7) ounces of red (MC) and 7(7,8) ounces of white (CC)
Circular knitting needles—sizes 7 and 9 or size needed to obtain correct gauge
Three stitch holders
Stitch markers
Tapestry needle
Six 1/2-inch white buttons
Red all-purpose thread

Hand-sewing needle
Scissors

Gauge: Using size 9 needles and St st, 7 sts and 10 rows = 2 inches.

Finished Size: Directions are for a Child size Small (4-6) with a chest measurement of about 29 inches and a length measurement of about 20 inches. Changes for sizes Medium (8-10) and Large (12-14) are in parentheses.

Stitches Used:
STOCKINETTE STITCH: St st
   Row 1 and all odd rows: K across row.
   Row 2 and all even rows: P across row.
   Repeat Rows 1 and 2.
KNIT 1, PURL 1 RIBBING: K1, p1 rib
   Row 1: * K 1, p 1; repeat from * across row.
   Row 2: * P 1, k 1; repeat from * across row.

Directions:
With smaller needles and MC, cast on 101(113,119) sts.
   Ribbing: Row 1: K 5 for front band, work in k 1, p 1 rib across row to last 5 sts, k 5 for front band.
   Row 2: K 5 for front band, work in p 1, k 1 rib across row to last 5 sts, k 5 for front band.
   Repeat Rows 1-2 until ribbing measures 2 in., ending with Row 2.
   For next row, k 5, work in k 1, p 1 rib, inc 12 sts evenly spaced across row to last 5 sts, k 5: 113(125,131) sts.
   BODY: With larger needles, k 5 in

MC for front band, join CC and work Row 1 of Pattern One in St st as shown on chart, starting at A, repeating pattern from A to B across row and ending at C, k 5 in MC for other side of front band. It will be necessary to join another strand of MC to work the front bands unless you carry the MC across the CC rows to work the front bands.
   Continue working Rows 1-10 of Pattern One until piece measures approximately 11-1/2(13-1/2,14-1/2) in., ending with Row 10 of pattern. Front bands continue to be knit every row.
   Break off MC used in Pattern One and work in CC for three rows, keeping front band in MC as before and ending on WS.
   Armhole: Work across the first 25 (29,30) sts, bind off next 10 sts for bottom of armhole, work across next 43(47,51) sts, bind off next 10 sts for bottom of armhole, work across remaining 25(29,30) sts. Place sts on holder to be worked later for yoke.
   SLEEVE (make two): Using smaller needles and MC, cast on 30(32,32) sts and work in rib until piece measures 2 in., ending with Row 2.
   For next row, inc 7(5,5) sts evenly spaced across row: 37(37,37) sts.
   With larger needles, join CC and work Row 1 of Pattern One in St st as shown on chart, starting at A, repeating pattern from A to B across row and ending at C.
   Repeat Rows 1-10 of Pattern One in St st, inc 2 sts each side of piece every fourth row 10(11,12) times. (Increased stitches are worked into a continuation of Pattern One.)
   Work even on these 57(59,61) sts until piece measures approximately 12(13,14) in. or desired length to armhole, ending on Row 10 of Pattern One.
   Break off MC used in Pattern One and work in CC for three rows, keeping front band in MC as before and ending on WS.
   At the start of next two rows, bind off 5 sts for underarm. Place 47(49,51) sts on holder to be worked later for the yoke.

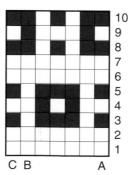

PATTERN ONE CHART

10
9
8
7
6
5
4
3
2
1

C B   A

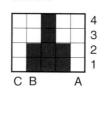

PATTERN TWO CHART

4
3
2
1

C B   A

ABBREVIATIONS
dec	decrease
inc	increase
k	knit
p	purl
RS	right side
st(s)	stitch(es)
tog	together
WS	wrong side

Repeat for second sleeve.

YOKE: Assemble sweater pieces on larger needles RS out as follows: Slide the 25(29,30) sts of right front onto needle, place marker, add the 47(49,51) sts of right sleeve, place marker, add the 43(47,51) back sts, place marker, add the 47(49,51) sts of left sleeve, place marker, add the 25(29-30) sts of left front: 187(203,213) sts.

Row 1: RS, for Large size only, k 5 in MC, k across row in CC to second marker, slip marker, k 2 tog, continue across row to 2 sts before third marker, k 2 tog and k across row in CC to last 5 sts, k 5 in MC.

For sizes Small and Medium, k 5 in MC, work across row in CC, slipping markers but not decreasing to last 5 sts, k 5 In MC: 187(203,211) sts.

Row 2: K 5 in MC, p across row in CC, slipping markers to last 5 sts, k 5 in MC.

Row 3: K 5 in MC, work Row 1 of Pattern Two in St st, starting at A, repeating pattern from A to B across row and ending at C, k last 5 sts in MC. At same time, make yoke decreases by knitting 2 sts tog before and after each of the four markers: 179(195,203) sts.

Row 4: Work Row 2 of Pattern Two in St st, starting at C and repeating pattern from B to A across row, ending at A.

Work Rows 3-4 of Pattern Two as before. Continue repeating the four rows of Pattern Two until four repeats have been completed, making decreases by knitting 2 sts tog before and after each of the four markers every k row, maintaining pattern as best you can with the decreases.

Work two rows of MC in St st, making decreases and working front bands as before.

Work Rows 3-4 and then Rows 1-2 of Pattern Two in St st, making decreases and working front bands as before. Fasten off MC for front bands.

Continue working Pattern Two, making decreases without working front bands, until 99(107,107) sts remain, ending on WS.

NECK: K 5 and place sts on holder. Continue across row in pattern, working decreases as before to last 5 sts, k 5 and place last 5 sts on holder.

Continue with pattern and decrease each k row as before, and at the same time, decrease 1 st at neck edge each side every other row three times until 35(43,43) sts remain: 0(3,3) right front sts, 13 right sleeve sts, 9(11,11) back sts, 13 left sleeve sts, 0(3,3) left front sts. End on WS and fasten off CC.

NECK RIBBING: Using MC and smaller needles, with RS facing, pick up and k across 5 right front band sts, pick up 14 sts from right band to sleeve, k across 35(43,43) body sts from needle, pick up 14 sts from left sleeve to left front band, k across 5 left band sts: 73(81,81) sts.

K every row of 5 sts of the left and the right front bands and work rest of the sts in k 1, p 1 rib until the ribbing measures 1-1/2 in., ending on WS. Bind off from RS in rib.

FINISHING: With right sides together, sew underarms of sleeves. Pull all of the yarn ends to WS and weave in the loose ends.

Mark location for six buttonholes evenly spaced on right band for a girl's sweater and on left band for a boy's sweater. Spread a space large enough for each button and stitch ends with red thread to secure opening.

Using red thread, sew buttons on other band to correspond with buttonholes.

Give to your favorite youngster! 🔔

Skier'll Swoosh into Your Heart

NATURALLY, you'll want to get cracking on this cute wintertime figure. "He's made with an acorn and sweet gum ball," explains Rose Pirrone of Bayside, New York. "Everyone who sees my trim just adores him!"

Best of all, he's well equipped for "travel" and glides easily from tree ornament to stand-alone figure.

Materials Needed:
One acorn
One sweet gum ball
One red bump chenille stem
One 3/8-inch red pom-pom
Two round toothpicks
Two craft (Popsicle) sticks
8 inches of worsted-weight yarn in color of choice for scarf
10 inches of gold metallic thread for hanger (optional)
Wire cutters
Craft scissors or X-acto knife
Glue gun and glue stick

Finished Size: Acorn skier is about 3 inches tall x 4-1/4 inches long.

Directions:
Use craft scissors or X-acto knife to cut one end of each craft stick in a V-shape for front of skis.

Referring to photo for placement, glue side of acorn to sweet gum ball for head. Then glue pom-pom to acorn.

For optional hanger, wrap metallic thread around neck and tie ends in a knot in back close to neck. Then tie ends together, leaving a loop for hanger.

Tie yarn around neck for scarf.

Use wire cutter to cut chenille stem into four pieces, leaving one narrow end and one rounded end on each piece as shown in Fig. 1.

Glue a rounded end of a chenille piece to each side of sweet gum ball body for arms, leaving narrow ends free.

Wrap narrow end of each arm around a toothpick for ski poles.

Glue rounded end of each remain-

ing chenille piece to bottom of body for legs. Bend narrow ends slightly to form feet. Glue bottom of each foot to a craft stick ski as shown in photo. Shape arms and legs as shown in photo.

Glide him right into your decor! 🔔

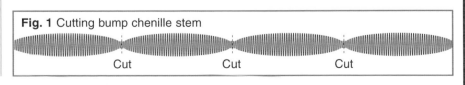

Fig. 1 Cutting bump chenille stem

Cut   Cut   Cut

Spiffy Sacks Put Fun Face on Gift-Giving

DELIVER good cheer by packing your presents in these fanciful bags. Both the bearded Santa and smiling snowman will figure plenty of extra fun into your festivities!

Crafter Kaci Ogg of Omaha, Nebraska came up with the idea, using run-of-the-mill bags and a little imagination. "Kids especially like this project," she notes. "They can help Mom by gluing on pom-poms, felt pieces and yarn."

Materials Needed (for both):
Patterns on next page
Tracing paper and pencil
Scissors
White (tacky) glue

Materials Needed (for Santa):
Acrylic craft paints—flesh, red and white
Paintbrushes—small flat and small round
Black medium-point permanent marker
1/2-inch red pom-pom for nose
3/4-inch white button
6-inch x 1-1/2-inch piece of white plush felt for fur trim on hat
9 yards of white yarn
6-inch square of heavy cardboard
11-inch-tall x 6-inch-wide x 3-1/2-inch-deep red heavy-weight paper gift bag

Materials Needed (for snowman):
Felt—1-3/4-inch square of orange for nose and 3-1/2-inch square of pink for cheeks
Seven 3/4-inch black pom-poms for eyes and mouth
7-inch x 10-inch piece of black and red plaid fabric for hat and scarf
Matching all-purpose thread
Hand-sewing needle
11-inch-tall x 6-inch-wide x 3-1/2-inch-deep white heavy-weight paper gift bag

Finished Size: Each gift bag is about 11 inches tall x 6 inches wide x 3-1/2 inches deep.

Directions:
SANTA: Trim open end of red gift bag as shown in Fig. 1.

Trace Santa's face pattern onto tracing paper. Cut out pattern.

Center the pattern on side of red gift bag with bottom edge of face pattern about 2-1/4 in. from bottom of gift bag. Trace around pattern with pencil.

Use flat brush and flesh to paint Santa's face. Let dry.

Turn pattern over and rub pencil over eyes on pattern to darken. Place pattern over Santa's face. Trace over lines of eyes to transfer pattern onto bag.

Use round brush to paint white portion of eyes. Let dry.

Use black marker to fill in lower portion of each eye. Then outline upper portion of each eye with black.

With a nearly dry brush and a circular motion, add red cheeks.

Glue red pom-pom nose to face between cheeks.

Cut fourteen 1-in.-long pieces of yarn and forty 4-in.-long pieces of yarn for Santa's hair. Glue short pieces to straight edge along top of Santa's face. Glue 20 of the longer pieces to each side of Santa's face, making sure top ends of all pieces of yarn are even.

Cut a 6-in.-long piece of yarn and set it aside. Wrap remaining yarn around cardboard square for Santa's mustache. Slip yarn off cardboard. Knot 6-in. piece of yarn around center of loops.

Glue center of mustache below nose.

Glue the felt strip across gift bag for the fur trim of Santa's hat, covering top ends of yarn pieces and leaving about 1/2 in. of yarn showing along the top of Santa's face.

Glue button to tip of hat.

SNOWMAN: Trim open end of white gift bag as shown in Fig. 2.

Cut cheeks and nose from felt as directed on patterns.

From plaid fabric, cut one 7-in. x 6-in. piece for hat, one 1-1/2-in. x 6-in. strip for scarf and one 1-1/2-in. x 7-in. strip for tie of scarf.

Thread hand-sewing needle with double strand of thread. Sew across one

Fig. 1 Trimming Santa gift bag

5 in.

Cut

Fig. 2 Trimming snowman gift bag

4 in.

Cut

Cut

2 in.

6-in. edge of hat piece about 3/8 in. from raw edge with running stitch for top of hat. See Fig. 3 for stitch illustration. Draw up thread until top of hat fits top edge of gift bag. Fasten off thread.

Fold under sides of hat about 1/2 in. Glue gathered top of hat to one side of gift bag with top of hat even with top of gift bag. Glue folded edges of hat to trimmed sides of gift bag.

Glue 6-in.-long strip to bottom of gift bag for scarf. Tie remaining strip in a knot. Glue knot to right edge of scarf.

Referring to photo for position, glue two pom-poms to gift bag for eyes. Glue cheeks and nose below eyes and remaining pom-poms for mouth to gift bag.

SNOWMAN PATTERNS

SANTA FACE PATTERN
Trace 1—tracing paper
Paint as directed

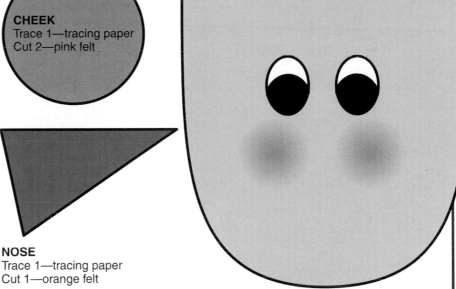

CHEEK
Trace 1—tracing paper
Cut 2—pink felt

NOSE
Trace 1—tracing paper
Cut 1—orange felt

Fig. 3 Running stitch

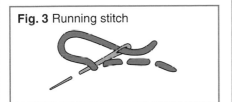

Red Wagon Holds Loads of Joy

HAULING in Noel appeal is what this nostalgic wagon does best! You can use it to decorate the hallway or a doorstep, or fill it with gifts and put it beneath the tree.

"The wagon's simple to make with a vegetable crate from the grocery store," assures Cyndee Kromminga from Winfield, Kansas. "If you can't find one, fashion your own from wood boards."

Add a coat of crimson paint, rope handle and four well-rounded wheels, and you're ready to roll!

Materials Needed:
17-3/8-inch-long x 14-inch-wide x 6-inch-high wooden vegetable crate*
27 inches of 1 x 8 pine (actual size 3/4 inch x 7-1/4 inches) for wheels
29 inches of 1 x 2 pine (actual size 3/4 inch x 1-1/2 inches) for axles
Scroll or band saw
Compass and pencil
Drill with 3/32-inch, 5/32-inch and 1/4-inch bits
Sandpaper and tack cloth
Gloss spray paint—black and red
Wood screws—four 3/4 inch and four 1-1/2-inch
Screwdriver
24 inches of 6-ply jute string

* Wooden vegetable crates are available from produce departments of most grocery stores. Or you can make your own, following the dimensions given and referring to the photo here.

Finished Size: Wagon measures 17-3/8 inches long x 15 inches wide x 9-3/8 inches high.

Directions:
Use compass to draw four 6-in. circles onto 1 x 8 pine for wheels. Use scroll or band saw to cut out each.

Sand wheels smooth and wipe with tack cloth to remove sanding dust.

Cut two 14-1/2-in.-long pieces from 1 x 2 pine for axles. If you made your own wooden crate, cut axles so they extend just beyond side edges of crate. Drill 3/32-in. holes into ends of each axle.

Spray entire crate red. Spray wheels and axles black. Let dry.

Position an axle on bottom (outside) of crate 3 in. from each narrow end. Working from inside of crate, drill pilot holes with 3/32-in. bit through bottom of crate and into axles about 2 in. from each end. Attach axles to bottom of crate with 3/4-in. screws.

Drill 5/32-in. holes through center of each wheel. Center wheels over ends of

axles and use 1-1/2-in. wood screws to attach a wheel to the end of each axle.

Drill two 1/4-in. holes centered 1 in. apart through front of wagon. Thread ends of jute string through holes from inside to outside of crate. Knot ends of jute string together about 1 in. from ends.

Fill with fun decorations! 🔔

Crocheted Coasters Are Aswirl in Nostalgia

LOVELY AND LACY, these crocheted coasters will lend an old-fashioned air to any setting for the holidays. Even better, the simple circlets are a delight to make, assures Darlene Polachic.

She crafted this set to brighten her Saskatoon, Saskatchewan home in just a few short hours, noting, "Anyone who's done some crocheting before will find the coasters quick and easy to complete."

Materials Needed (for all):
Size 10 crochet cotton—one ball each of green, red and white
Size 5 steel crochet hook
Tapestry needle
Scissors

Finished Size: Each coaster measures about 4-1/4 inches across.

Directions:
With white, ch 7, sl st into first ch to form a ring.

Round 1: Ch 4 for first tr, work 23 trs in ring, join with sl st to fourth ch of beginning ch-4: 24 trs.

Round 2: Ch 4, * work 1 dc in next tr, ch 1; repeat from * around, join with sl st in third ch of beginning ch-4: 24 ch-sps.

Round 3: Sl st into next ch-sp, ch 5, * work 1 dc in next ch-sp, ch 2; repeat from * around, join with sl st in third ch of beginning ch-5.

Round 4: Sl st into next ch-sp, ch 3, work 1 dc in same sp, * ch 1, work 2 dcs in next ch-2 sp; repeat from * around, ch 1, join with sl st in third ch of beginning ch-3.

Round 5: Sl st to next ch-sp, ch 3, work 1 dc in same ch-sp, * ch 2, work 2 dcs in next ch-sp; repeat from * around, ch 2, join with sl st in third ch of beginning ch-3.

Round 6: Sl st to next ch-sp, ch 3, work 1 dc in same ch-sp, * ch 3, work 2 dcs in next ch-sp; repeat from * around, ch 3, join with sl st in third ch of beginning ch-3.

Round 7: Sl st to next ch-sp, ch 3, work 2 dcs in same ch-sp, * ch 2, work 3 dcs in next ch-sp; repeat from * around, ch 2, join with sl st in third ch of beginning ch-3.

Round 8: Sl st to next ch-sp, ch 3, work 3 dcs in same ch-sp, * ch 2, work 4 dcs in next ch-sp; repeat from * around, ch 3, join with sl st in third ch of beginning ch-3.

Round 9: Sl st to next ch-sp, ch 5, work 1 dc in same ch-sp, * ch 5, (dc, ch 2, dc) in next ch-sp; repeat from * around, ending with ch 5, join with sl st in third ch of beginning ch-5. Fasten off.

EDGING: Attach red or green with sc in any ch 2-sp, work 2 more scs in same ch-sp, * ch 5, work 3 scs in next ch 5-sp, ch 5, work 3 scs in next ch 2-sp; repeat from * around, join with sl st in first sc. Fasten off.

Use a tapestry needle to weave in the loose ends.

Place your coasters on tables and watch them soak up compliments! 🔔

ABBREVIATIONS

ch(s)	chain(s)
dc(s)	double crochet(s)
sc(s)	single crochet(s)
sl st	slip stitch
sp(s)	space(s)
tr(s)	treble crochet(s)

Angels Bring in Christmas Cheer

THESE lacy angels will spread smiles all around! Irma Fredrickson of Stewartville, Minnesota, who fashioned the delicate decorations from paper doilies and clothespins, notes that youngsters especially enjoy tackling them.

Quick to craft, the festive figures will be all aglow if you doll them up in gold or silver doilies, she also points out.

Then hang them on the tree or showcase in a seasonal centerpiece.

Materials Needed (for both):
8-inch round paper doily with medallion design for large angel
6-inch round paper doily with medallion design for small angel
3-3/4-inch-long wooden slotted clothespin or doll pin for large angel
2-1/2-inch-long x 1/4-inch-thick wooden slotted (baby flat) clothespin for small angel
White (tacky) glue
Scissors

Finished Size: Large angel is about 4-1/2 inches long x 6 inches across. Small angel is about 3 inches across.

Directions:
LARGE ANGEL: Carefully cut out center medallion from 8-in. paper doily. Set aside for use later.

Fold doily in half to make a half circle and crease along fold. Open doily and cut on crease, making two half circles. Set one half circle aside for another project.

Fold the remaining half circle in half and crease along the fold. Open the doily and cut on the crease, making two triangular sections.

For angel's dress, carefully wrap one triangle section around 3-3/4-in.-long clothespin or doll pin with right side of doily facing out. Glue straight edges of doily to edges of slots on clothespin, leaving top of clothespin exposed for head. Let dry.

For wings, fold remaining triangle about 1 in. from tip. Glue wings centered onto back of clothespin with fold of wings even with top of dress as shown in photo. Let dry.

Glue medallion centered onto back of head of angel. Let dry.

SMALL ANGEL: Follow instructions for large angel, using 6-in. paper doily and 2-1/2-in.-long clothespin instead.

Add spirit to your home with these beauties!

HALF the fun of the holiday season is making merry Christmas crafts. But without a little planning, those craft projects can become more of a burden instead of a joy to behold.

To keep your Yuletide crafting spirited and *not* a race with the clock, follow these handy tips from Craft Editor Jane Craig:

● Jot down a schedule on your calendar. Calculate how long you'll need for each project.

● Begin early. Don't wait until a week before Christmas to get to work. Even Santa's efficient elves need more time than that!

● Set a deadline after which you will not start any new holiday project—and stick to it!

Simple Santa Shares Yule Spirit

GIVING the gift of good cheer is in the bag with this festive Father Christmas. "He's eye-catching and easy to make," mentions Patricia Klesh of Martinsville, New Jersey.

What's more, the sturdy Santa stands perfectly on a mantel or shelf and makes a wonderful stocking stuffer. "All he takes to make is a cardboard cone, paint, pipe cleaners and other simple supplies," Patricia points out.

Materials Needed:
4-inch-high Styrofoam or cardboard cone
2-inch Styrofoam ball
Acrylic craft paints—flesh and red
Small flat paintbrush
18 inches of white loopy jumbo chenille or white curly doll hair
Five 6mm white pipe cleaners (chenille stems)
One green bump chenille stem
1/2-inch white pom-pom
Two 7mm glue-on wiggle eyes
Purchased 3/4-inch-high x 3/4-inch-wide wrapped gift box
6-inch square of red felt
Miniature silk holly leaves with berries
Ruler or tape measure
Quilter's marking pen or pencil
Glue gun and glue sticks
Scissors

Finished Size: Cone Santa is about 7 inches tall x 3 inches wide.

Directions:
Paint Styrofoam or cardboard cone red and Styrofoam ball flesh. Let dry.

Glue ball to top of cone for head.

Glue two white 6mm pipe cleaners down front of cone as shown in photo, leaving about 1/2 in. between pipe cleaners at bottom. Trim excess.

Fold and glue two white pipe cleaners in a 3/4-in.-high zigzag pattern around the base of cone as shown in the photo.

Cut two bumps from green bump chenille stem. Fold each in half for mittens. Wrap and glue a 1-in. length of white pipe cleaner around ends of each for cuff.

Glue mittens to sides of cone about 1/2 in. from top. Glue wrapped gift between hands as shown in photo.

Glue wiggle eyes to head. Remove a holly berry from silk holly and glue it to head below eyes for Santa's nose.

Cut a 1-in. length of loopy chenille and glue under Santa's nose for beard. Or glue doll hair under nose for beard.

Cut a 6-in. length and an 11-in. length of loopy chenille for Santa's hair. Glue longer piece centered across top of head with ends at each side. Fold shorter piece gently in half. Glue fold to back of head with all ends even. Or glue doll hair to head for Santa's hair.

Place square of felt on a flat surface. Measure and mark an arc with quilter's marking pen or pencil 5 in. from one corner as shown in Fig. 1. Cut along marked line. Overlap straight edges about 1/4 in. and glue to form a cone for Santa's hat.

Glue a white pipe cleaner around bottom edge of hat. Trim excess. Glue pom-pom to tip of hat. Glue hat to top

of Santa's head. Shape hat as shown in photo. Glue holly to edge of hat.

Set Santa out—and watch him wrap up smiles!

Fig. 1 Cutting Santa's hat

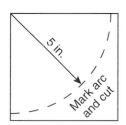

5 in.

Mark arc and cut

Spruced-Up Baskets Are Brimming with Yule Flavor

WEAVE some fun into your holidays with these attractive country baskets from crafter Jodi Shebester of Concord, North Carolina.

The designs are easy to follow and so decorative they're perfect for any room in your house. Fill them with utensils...tuck in a few small evergreen boughs...pour in yummy candies...or add anything you like!

Materials Needed (for each basket):
*Natural reed—1/2-inch flat for stakes and 1/4-inch flat for weavers
Green or red reed*—No. 2 or 3 round for twining the base and rim
Heavy scissors or side cutters
Tape measure
Pencil
Large plastic bucket to soak reed
Old towel
Spring-type clothespins
Needle-nose pliers*

Materials Needed (for trims):
Dark red and yellow acrylic paints,
*small flat paintbrush and toothpick for poinsettia basket
3-inch-high tie-on ceramic Christmas tree trim and 6 inches of 1/8-inch-wide green satin ribbon, or 3-inch-high dark green wooden tree cutout and white (tacky) glue for Christmas tree basket*

*To dye your own materials, use red or green Rit dye and follow the instructions included in the package.

Shopping Information: To order kits for these baskets, write The Basket House, Gerda Jodi Shebester, 527 Union Street South, Concord NC 28025-5570 or phone 1-704/782-5993.

The cost, $10.00 for the Poinsettia basket and $13.00 for the Christmas tree basket, includes shipping.

Finished Size: Each basket is about 6 inches tall x 3-3/4 inches across.

Directions:
For stakes, cut six 21-in.-long pieces of 1/2-in. natural reed.

Soak reed in warm water until pliable. Measure and mark the centers on rough side of stakes.

Place towel on a flat surface. Lay out the six pieces rough side up as shown in Fig. 1. Adjust base to 2-in. square.

BASKET: Twining the base: Soak the green or red round reed until pliable. Remove from water and wipe with towel to remove excess dye from reed.

Place ends of piece together to find center. Use needle-nose pliers to make a crimp about 3 in. from center. Loop the crimped spot around one of the stakes.

Twine for two rows with green or red round reed. See Fig. 2. These rows of twining form part of the base of the basket. Do not end the twine.

Upsetting the stakes: Working with dampened basket base, gently bend each stake upward from the base by rolling the stakes over your finger. Hold in place with clothespins as needed.

At end of second row, add another piece of matching round reed to continue twining. Triple twine for four or five rows as follows: Pick up piece of reed to far left and bring it in front of the next two stakes, behind the third and then out to the front. See Fig. 3.

Continue weaving in front of two and behind one for desired number of rows. There should never be two pieces of reed coming out of the same slot. Tuck ends in and trim.

Sides: Split one stake on basket in half lengthwise to allow for continuous weaving.

Soak 1/4-in. natural reed until pliable.

Taper one end of reed. Place the tapered end to the inside behind a stake and weave around stakes continuously until basket is about 5 in. tall.

Keep stakes vertical and pack weaving down closely after each row, making sure that all sides of basket are vertical, corners are gently rounded and base is flat. Remove clothespins as you weave, replacing them if needed.

On last round, taper end as in the beginning so top of basket is level.

Twining the top: Prepare matching round reed as before. Insert three weavers into three spaces next to each other. Triple twine for four or five rows as before. Tuck ends in and trim.

When finished twining, dampen stakes until pliable. Then tuck stakes down and tuck ends into 1/4-in. reed on inside, bypassing twining at the top.

FINISHING: Poinsettia: Cut four 3-in.-long pieces of 1/4-in. natural reed. Paint all sides of each piece dark red. Let dry.

Find the center of the best side of

your basket. To add poinsettia trim as shown in photo, count seven rows of 1/4-in. reed up from bottom of basket and insert a piece of painted reed behind stakes to left and right of center reed.

Add a diagonal piece from left top to right bottom and another diagonal piece from left bottom to right top. Then add final vertical piece.

Dip toothpick into yellow paint and dab several tiny dots onto center of poinsettia trim. Let dry.

Insert matching round reed behind stakes and over two rows of 1/4-in. reed, making curls as shown in photo.

Christmas tree: Thread ribbon from front to back through holes in ceramic Christmas tree. Then thread ribbon through reed from outside to inside on center of best side of basket. Tie ends on inside of basket to secure. Or glue wooden tree cutout to basket.

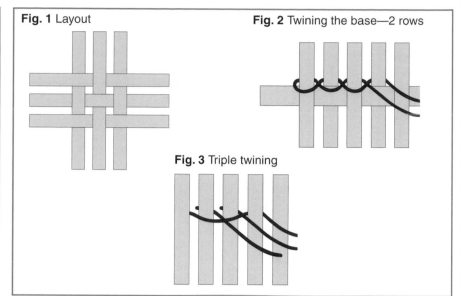

Fig. 1 Layout

Fig. 2 Twining the base—2 rows

Fig. 3 Triple twining

Accents Carry Merry Messages

FILLED with holiday sentiment, these adorable crocheted trims from Beverly Mewhorter of Apache Junction, Arizona help bring home the meaning of Christmas.

Using basic crochet stitches, Beverly created the diamond shapes, then painted on words suited for the season.

You can quickly do the same, thanks to her easy instructions here. You can also add family names to personalize the trims.

Materials Needed:
4-ply worsted-weight yarn—1.5 ounces of red and small amount of green
Size G/6 (4.25mm) crochet hook
Polyester stuffing
Gold dimensional paint
Tapestry needle
Scissors

Finished Size: Each ornament measures about 4 inches square without the hanger and tassel.

Directions:
SIDES (make two): Row 1: With red yarn, ch 13, sc in second ch from hk and in each ch across, ch 1, turn.

Rows 2-12: Sc in each st across, ch 1, turn. Fasten off at end of Row 12.

TO JOIN: Hold two sides together with sts and ends of rows matching. Working through both layers, join green yarn with a sl st in any st, sc in each st or end of row around, working three scs in corners and inserting stuffing before closing, join with sl st to first st.

HANGING LOOP: Join green yarn with a sl st in any corner, ch 12, sl st in beginning st. Fasten off.

TASSEL: Cut eight 5-in.-long pieces of green yarn. Working with all strands as one, fold yarn in half.

Insert crochet hook in corner opposite hanging loop. Draw fold of yarn through corner to make loop. Bring yarn ends through loop and pull ends to tighten loop around yarn. Trim ends even.

Repeat two more times to make three pillows.

FINISHING: Use paint to write on trims as shown in photo. Let dry.

Soften your surroundings with these cushy trims!

ABBREVIATIONS	
ch(s)	chains
hk	hook
sc(s)	single crochet(s)
sl st	slip stitch
st(s)	stitch(es)

Santa Shines Bright on Pines

STARSTRUCK—that's what guests will be when they catch sight of this smiling Claus on your Christmas tree!

Ann Lischka crafted the plastic canvas character to enliven her Lowell, Wisconsin home for the holidays and shares her easy instructions here so you can do the same. "The loop stitch I used for Santa's beard is lots of fun to do," she adds.

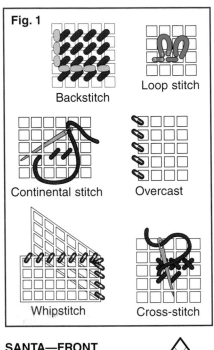

Fig. 1

Backstitch

Loop stitch

Continental stitch

Overcast

Whipstitch

Cross-stitch

SANTA—FRONT
Stitch 1—as shown
SANTA—BACK
Stitch 1—as directed

Materials Needed:
Charts on this page
7-count clear plastic canvas—two 5-inch star shapes for Santa's body and one 6-inch square for boots, mittens and hat
Worsted-weight yarn—5 yards of black, 1 yard of light peach, 1/2 yard of gold, 3 yards of green, 1/2 yard of light blue, 1/2 yard of pink, 15 yards of red and 6 yards of white
Size 16 tapestry needle
Polyester stuffing
3/8-inch white pom-pom
White (tacky) glue
18 inches of 18-gauge craft wire for hanger
18 inches of multicolor star garland for hanger
Scissors

Finished Size: Star Santa measures about 6-3/4 inches across x 6-1/2 inches high without hanger.

Directions:
CUTTING: Remembering to count bars and not holes, cut boots, mittens, hat and tip of hat following charts.

STITCHING: Working with 18-in. to 20-in. lengths of yarn, refer to charts and instructions to stitch pieces. See Fig. 1 for stitch illustrations.

Do not knot yarn on back of work.

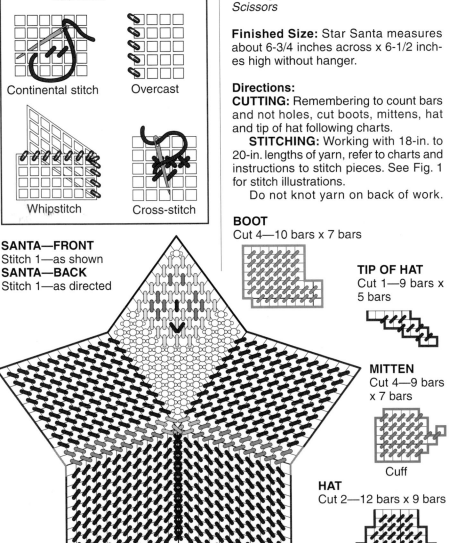

BOOT
Cut 4—10 bars x 7 bars

TIP OF HAT
Cut 1—9 bars x 5 bars

MITTEN
Cut 4—9 bars x 7 bars

Cuff

HAT
Cut 2—12 bars x 9 bars

Instead, leave a 1-in. tail on back of plastic canvas and work the next few stitches over it. To end a strand, run yarn under completed stitches of the same color and clip yarn close to work.

Boots (stitch four, reversing two): Use black yarn and Continental stitch to fill in boots as shown on chart. Overcast top edges but omit whipstitching.

Place two boots together with wrong sides facing and edges matching. Whipstitch around sides and bottom of boot with black yarn where shown on chart, leaving tops open. Repeat with remaining two boots.

Mittens (stitch four, reversing two): Use green yarn and Continental stitch to fill in mittens as shown on chart. Overcast cuff edges but omit whipstitching.

PLASTIC CANVAS SANTA COLOR AND STITCH KEY
CONTINENTAL STITCH
- Black
- Light peach
- Gold
- Green
- Light blue
- Pink
- Red

BACKSTITCH
- Red

CROSS-STITCH
- Gold
- Red

LOOP STITCH
- White

WHIPSTITCH
- Black
- Green
- Red
- White

OVERCAST
- Black
- Green
- Red

Place two mittens together with wrong sides facing and edges matching. Whipstitch around mitten with green yarn where shown on chart, leaving cuff ends open. Repeat with remaining two mittens.

Hat (stitch two): Use red yarn and Continental stitch to fill in hat pieces as shown on chart, omitting whipstitching.

Place hat pieces together with wrong sides facing and edges matching. Whipstitch sides of hat with red yarn where shown on chart, leaving bottom of hat open and top unstitched.

Tip of hat: Use red yarn and Continental stitch to fill in tip of hat as shown on chart. Overcast around tip of hat and whipstitch bottom edge to top of hat piece with red yarn, stitching through all three layers.

Santa: Following direction of stitching as shown on chart, stitch front of Santa with Continental stitch as follows:

Fill in buckle with gold yarn and belt with black yarn; stitch arms and legs with red yarn; stitch cheeks with pink yarn, eyes with blue yarn and nose with red yarn; and fill in face with light peach yarn.

Separate the plies of red yarn and use a single ply to backstitch mouth.

Stitch Santa's hair, beard and mustache with white yarn and loop stitch, making 1/4-in.-long loops.

Stitch back of Santa following instructions for front of Santa, omitting instructions for buckle and face. Fill in buckle area with black yarn and Continental stitch and entire face area with white yarn and loop stitch.

Hold front and back of Santa togeth-er with wrong sides facing and edges matching. Whipstitch all sides together with matching yarn, adding stuffing between the layers as you stitch.

Cut through the loop of each loop stitch. Then use needle to fluff yarn. Trim beard and hair to desired length.

FINISHING: Glue a boot over the end of each leg and a mitten over the end of each arm as shown in photo.

Glue hat onto top of Santa's head with tip of hat toward the front. Glue pom-pom to tip of hat.

Coil craft wire around pencil. Remove wire from pencil. Thread an end of wire through each of Santa's hands. Bend ends in a loop to secure. Stretch and shape wire over Santa's head from mitten to mitten for hanger.

Wrap star garland around hanger as shown in photo.

Door Decor Lines Up Happy Look

ASSEMBLED from simple supplies like ribbons and eyelet trim, this charming hanger will enhance your decorating in no time!

"I used what I had on hand to make it and was finished in an afternoon," details Lana Condon of Jupiter, Florida.

"The mini ornaments I glued on add a colorful touch, but if you don't have any, try attaching buttons or painted wooden cutouts instead."

Materials Needed:
20 inches of 1-1/2-inch-wide red grosgrain ribbon
1/2 yard of 3/4-inch-wide green, red and white embroidered ribbon
1/8-inch-wide satin ribbon—1 yard of red and 2-1/2 yards of green
3-inch x 3-1/2-inch purchased red and white check bow or 1/2 yard of 1-1/4-inch-wide red and white check ribbon to make bow
1 yard of 3-1/2-inch-wide white eyelet trim with one scalloped edge and one straight raw edge
All-purpose thread—green, red and white
1-inch gold jingle bell
1-1/4-inch-high Christmas trims or novelty buttons (Lana used stocking, snowman and candy cane trims)
3/4-inch plastic ring for hanger
White (tacky) glue
Standard sewing supplies

Finished Size: Ribbon hanging is about 5-1/2 inches wide x 22-1/2 inches long.

Directions:
Cut straight across each end of red grosgrain ribbon. Fold one cut end to one side of ribbon with cut edges meeting in center, forming a point. Hand-sew with red thread on back side to secure point for bottom of ribbon hanging.

Slip other end of ribbon through plastic ring and hand-sew end to wrong side of ribbon for hanger.

Cut eyelet trim into three 12-in.-long pieces. Fold and press 1/4 in. to wrong side on long raw edge and each short edge of each piece. Sew pressed edges with white thread.

Pleat long hemmed edge with 1/2-in. accordion pleats to make fans. Hand-sew through pleated end 1/2 in. from hem to hold.

Cut 3/4-in.-wide embroidered ribbon into three 6-in.-long pieces. Hand-sew running stitch close to one long edge of ribbon with matching thread, leaving thread attached. For stitch illustration, see Fig. 1 on page 103.

Pull thread to draw ribbon into a circle. Overlap ends and stitch to hold.

Cut red satin ribbon into three 12-in.-long pieces and green satin ribbon into six 12-in.-long pieces. Working with one red and two green ribbons as one, tie into a small bow as shown in photo. Repeat with remaining pieces.

Glue eyelet fan centered onto right

side of grosgrain ribbon. Glue remaining eyelet fans above and below center fan, leaving about 2-1/2 in. between fans.

Glue a ribbon circle to center bottom of each fan and a ribbon bow to center of each circle.

Glue or hand-sew trims or buttons below each fan as shown in photo.

Thread remaining green satin ribbon through top of jingle bell. Tie ribbon in a bow. Glue or hand-sew bow to bottom point of grosgrain ribbon.

Glue or hand-sew purchased or homemade red and white check bow to top, covering plastic ring.

Hang on the front door and ring in the holidays!

Felt Display Opens Door to Season's Meaning

SETTING THE SCENE for the real message Christmas brings is what this clever Nativity does for young and old alike, tells country crafter Jan Koepsell of Paonia, Colorado.

"I first made the fold-up creche for a nursing home resident who didn't have room for a big display," she relates. "Children also enjoy it because the soft sturdy characters can be moved around, thanks to Velcro strips I attached to their backs."

Materials Needed:
Patterns on next page
Tracing paper and pencil
Cardboard or poster board—two 5-1/2-inch x 8-1/2-inch pieces for folded front of stable and one 8-1/2-inch x 11-inch piece for back of stable
9-inch x 24-inch piece of brown print fabric for outside of stable
9-inch x 24-inch piece of tan fabric for inside of stable
1/2-inch-wide hook and loop tape— one 2-1/2-inch-long piece for front closure and ten 1/2-inch squares for attaching pieces
Felt scraps—two 3-inch x 3-3/4-inch pieces each of light blue for Mary, green, purple and red for kings, rust for one shepherd and tan for Joseph; one 3-inch square of black for heads of sheep; one 6-inch square of brown for other shepherd and cradle; one 6-inch square of off-white for all faces and hands; one 5-inch x 3-inch piece of gold for star and rays; and one 8-inch square of white for angel, wings, baby Jesus and sheep

Six-strand embroidery floss—black, brown, light blue, green, purple, red, rust, tan and white
Embroidery needle
Metallic trims—2 inches each of four different trims for angel and kings (Jan used rickrack, ribbon and gold cord)
Three small gold metallic beads for gifts
One gray pipe cleaner (chenille stem)
Polyester stuffing
White (tacky) glue
Transparent tape
All-purpose thread—brown, gold, tan and white
Standard sewing supplies

Finished Size: Felt Nativity measures about 21-1/2 inches across x 8 inches high when opened. Folded Nativity measures about 10-1/2 inches across x 8 inches high. Patterns of figures are actual size.

Directions:
FIGURES: Trace patterns onto tracing paper. Cut shapes from felt as directed on patterns.

Cut out circle from one felt shape to make opening for face of angel, baby, shepherds, kings, Mary and Joseph. Cut a 1-in. square of off-white felt for the face of each figure. Center and glue a face behind each opening, trimming away excess off-white felt as needed.

Separate six-strand embroidery floss and use one strand to add a red French knot nose and black French knot eyes to each face as shown on patterns. See Fig. 1 for stitch illustration.

Sew the hook side of a 1/2-in. piece of

hook and loop tape centered onto the back of each felt figure except the baby. Sew hook side of a 1/2-in. piece of hook and loop tape onto back of cradle.

Pin matching colors of felt figures together with wrong sides facing and edges matching.

Separate six-strand embroidery floss and use two strands of matching floss to blanket-stitch around each figure, adding stuffing as you stitch.

Pin front and back of cradle together with bottom and side edges matching. Use two strands of brown floss to stitch sides and bottom of cradle together with blanket stitch. Slip baby into cradle and stitch across front of cradle with brown floss and blanket stitch, catching baby in stitching to hold.

Referring to photo for placement, glue two hands to front of all figures except baby.

Glue metallic trim to the top of green, red and purple figures. Hand-sew or glue a bead between the hands of each.

Glue metallic trim to top of angel and wings to back as shown in photo.

Separate white six-strand embroidery floss and use one strand to add a French knot nose and eyes to each sheep head where shown on pattern.

Glue heads centered onto three sheep bodies. Sew a square of hook side of hook and loop tape centered onto back of remaining sheep body.

Pin a body with a head to remaining sheep body with wrong sides facing and edges matching. Blanket-stitch around body with two strands of floss, adding stuffing as you stitch.

STABLE: Trace stable pattern twice onto folded tracing paper as directed on pattern.

Cut one traced pattern in half on fold of pattern, making two pattern pieces for fronts of stable. Tape sides of fronts to sides of back for complete pattern. See Fig. 2. Cut one from tan fabric for inside of stable and one from brown print fabric for outside of stable.

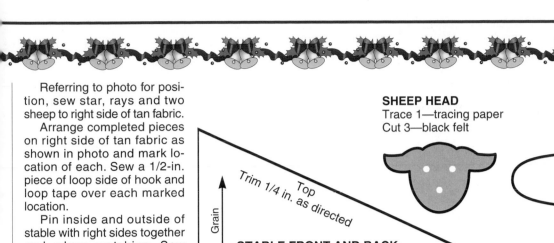

Referring to photo for position, sew star, rays and two sheep to right side of tan fabric.

Arrange completed pieces on right side of tan fabric as shown in photo and mark location of each. Sew a 1/2-in. piece of loop side of hook and loop tape over each marked location.

Pin inside and outside of stable with right sides together and edges matching. Sew along front opening and top with a 1/4-in. seam. Trim corners and turn right side out.

Trim 1/4 in. from top, bottom and front edges of pattern pieces where indicated on the pattern.

Remove tape and separate pattern pieces to make one pattern piece for back and two pieces for front of stable. Cut one each from cardboard or poster board.

Insert back and side pieces of cardboard or poster board between inside and outside layers of stable. Turn 1/4 in. to inside along bottom edge of fabric and hand-sew to secure.

Machine-stitch along front and back side edges, stitching between pieces of cardboard or poster board. Do not stitch through the cardboard or poster board.

For closure, sew loop side of hook and loop tape centered along one outside front edge of stable, stitching through fabric and cardboard.

Close stable as shown in photo and mark location of tape on inside front edge of other side. Sew hook side of tape to inside edge, stitching through fabric and cardboard.

Share the reason for the season with everyone in your family!

Fig 1

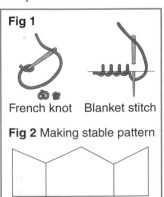

French knot   Blanket stitch

Fig 2 Making stable pattern

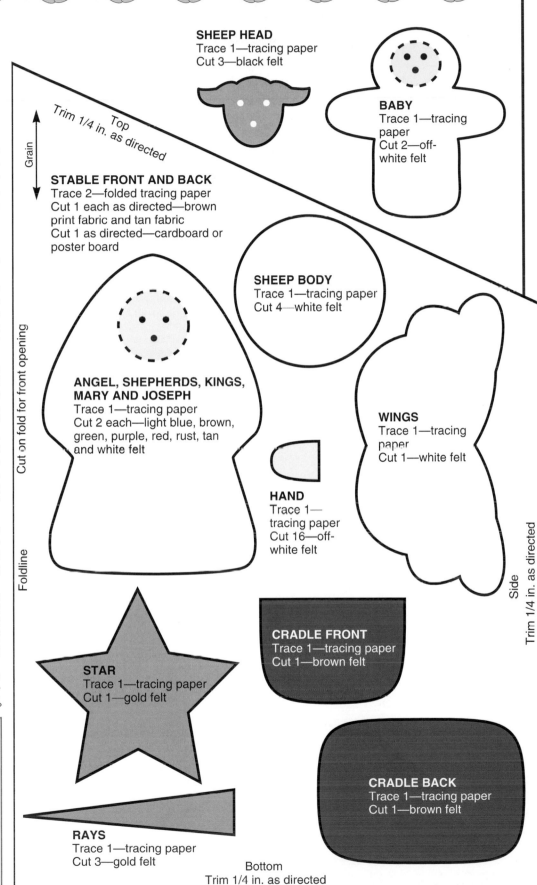

Grain

Top
Trim 1/4 in. as directed

SHEEP HEAD
Trace 1—tracing paper
Cut 3—black felt

BABY
Trace 1—tracing paper
Cut 2—off-white felt

STABLE FRONT AND BACK
Trace 2—folded tracing paper
Cut 1 each as directed—brown print fabric and tan fabric
Cut 1 as directed—cardboard or poster board

Cut on fold for front opening

Foldline

SHEEP BODY
Trace 1—tracing paper
Cut 4—white felt

ANGEL, SHEPHERDS, KINGS, MARY AND JOSEPH
Trace 1—tracing paper
Cut 2 each—light blue, brown, green, purple, red, rust, tan and white felt

HAND
Trace 1—tracing paper
Cut 16—off-white felt

WINGS
Trace 1—tracing paper
Cut 1—white felt

Side
Trim 1/4 in. as directed

STAR
Trace 1—tracing paper
Cut 1—gold felt

CRADLE FRONT
Trace 1—tracing paper
Cut 1—brown felt

CRADLE BACK
Trace 1—tracing paper
Cut 1—brown felt

RAYS
Trace 1—tracing paper
Cut 3—gold felt

Bottom
Trim 1/4 in. as directed

Her Candleholders Spark a Glow Everywhere They Go

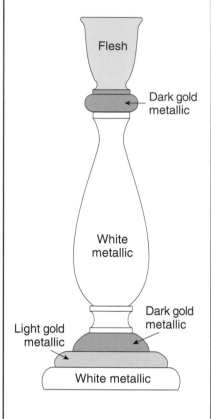

Fig. 1 Painting diagram

Flesh

Dark gold metallic

White metallic

White metallic

Dark gold metallic

Light gold metallic

White metallic

Fig. 2 Face painting pattern

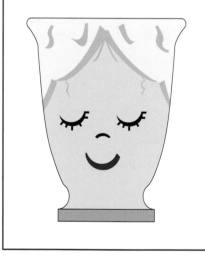

Acrylic craft paints—light gold metallic, dark gold metallic, white metallic, flesh and yellow (Fran used DecoArt Dazzling Metallic paints in Champagne Gold, Glorious Gold and Oyster Pearl and DecoArt Americana paints in Flesh Tone and Moon Yellow)
Paintbrushes—small flat and small round
White (tacky) glue
Clear acrylic spray sealer
Fine-line permanent markers—black and red
Two taper candles

Finished Size: Each candleholder measures about 6-3/4 inches tall x 3-3/4 inches across.

Directions:
Place small amounts of paint on paper plate or palette as needed. Paint all pieces as directed. Apply a second coat as needed for complete coverage, allowing drying time between each coat.

Use flat brush to paint all sides of each wooden heart dark gold metallic. Let dry.

Dip handle of brush into light gold metallic paint and dab dots onto outer edge on one side of each heart, placing dots a scant 1/4 in. from edge and about 1/4 in. apart. Let dry.

Referring to painting diagram, paint candleholders as follows: Paint rings at top and bottom of each candleholder dark gold as shown in photo. Let dry.

Use flat brush to paint each candle cup flesh. Let dry.

Use flat brush to paint bottom ring and body of candleholder white metallic. Let dry.

Use flat brush to paint middle ring on base of candleholder light gold metallic. Let dry.

Use flat brush to paint yellow hair on candle cup as shown in face painting pattern. Let dry.

Use round brush to add medium gold metallic streaks to hair. Let dry.

Glue the right side of a heart onto back of each candleholder with rounded

FOLKS will see the light when you set this cherubic pair out among your holiday accents!

To make them for her Albertville, Minnesota abode, Fran Farris turned to wooden candleholders, wooden hearts and acrylic paints. In a flash, you can finish up a twosome, too, thanks to the easy instructions she shares below.

Materials Needed (for both):
Two 6-3/4-inch-high wooden candleholders
Two brass inserts to fit candleholders
Two purchased 3-3/4-inch-wide x 3-inch-high x 1/8-inch-thick wooden hearts for wings
Paper plate or palette

portion up and point down for wings as shown in photo. Let dry.

Spray candleholders with acrylic sealer. Let dry.

Use markers to add a tiny red mouth and black eyes to face as shown in face painting pattern.

Glue a candle insert into each candle cup. Let dry.

Place a candle in each—and enjoy!

Miniature Evergreen Makes 'Scent'sational Noel Accent

HERE'S a fresh festive idea from Ellen Douglas of Cincinnati, Ohio—a country tree that smells as good as it looks. What's the secret? To craft it, she used an air freshener as a base for the balsam!

For the boughs, Ellen cut strips of fabric, then fashioned rustic decorations from buttons and bits of raffia. "The painted star I wired to the top adds the final fitting touch," she sums up about her aromatic idea. "It's easy and fun!"

Materials Needed:

Air freshener container (Ellen used a Renuzit adjustable air freshener container)
6-inch square of off-white fabric for tree trunk
8-inch x 17-inch piece of green print fabric for tree
Green all-purpose thread
Hand-sewing needle
Fifty 1/4-inch to 3/4-inch buttons in several different colors
Gold acrylic craft paint
Small flat paintbrush
One 1-1/2-inch-high x 1/16-inch-thick wooden star
12 inches of 20-gauge craft wire
Several strands of natural raffia
18 inches of 3-ply jute string
Glue gun and glue sticks
Scissors

Finished Size: Air freshener tree measures about 9 inches tall x 4 inches across.

Directions:

Paint all sides of star gold. Let dry.

Center base of air freshener on square of off-white fabric. Bring fabric up around base and glue to hold. Trim excess fabric even with top of base.

Wrap jute string around base and tie ends in a bow.

Cut or tear an 8-in. x 17-in. piece of green fabric into five 2-in.-wide strips measuring 17 in., 15 in., 13 in., 11 in. and 6 in. long. Fringe strips by making 1-in.-long cuts 1/2 in. apart along one long side of each strip.

Thread needle with a double strand of thread and knot ends together. Sew a running stitch 1/4 in. from unfringed edge of 17-in.-long strip. See Fig. 1 for stitch illustration. Draw up thread until strip is about 10 in. long. Fasten off

thread and distribute gathers evenly along strip.

Repeat, gathering 15-in. strip to 9 in., 13-in. strip to 7 in. and 11-in. strip to 5 in. Sew running stitch along unfringed edge of 6-in. strip, leaving thread attached. Draw up thread to form strip into a circle. Overlap ends and fasten off thread.

Glue gathered edge of longest strip around air freshener top so fringed edge of strip is even with bottom of base when container is closed as shown in Fig. 2. Overlap ends of strip and glue to hold.

Glue remaining strips to cone with fringed edge extending a bit over gathered edge of last strip, adding longest strip first. Then glue circle of fabric onto top of container.

Glue buttons randomly to fringe as shown in photo.

Cut several 4-in.-long pieces of raffia. Tie a knot in the center of each. Glue knots of raffia pieces randomly to gathered edge of strips, concealing knots under fringe. Trim ends of raffia to desired length.

Wrap craft wire around a pencil to coil wire. Remove pencil from wire. Then wrap center of wire around star as shown in Fig. 3, pulling ends of wire to stretch coil. Glue one end of wire to top of tree.

Tie a 10-in.-long piece of raffia in a

small bow. Glue bow to top of tree.

Plant your sweet-smelling evergreen among your holiday trims!

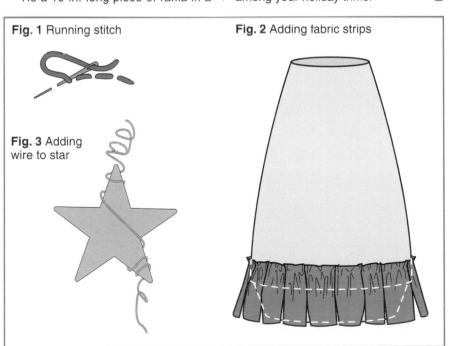

Fig. 1 Running stitch

Fig. 3 Adding wire to star

Fig. 2 Adding fabric strips

Crafty Family's Nicks Do More Than Deliver Gifts!

EVERYONE KNOWS what Santa Claus does each Christmas Eve. But how does the jolly old elf occupy his time the other 364 days of the year?

"He plays golf…engineers trains…uses a laptop computer…and paddles a wooden canoe," grins Carol Vance of rural Benton, Pennsylvania, as she carefully poses a handcrafted Kris.

"Also—as my family imagines it—the merry guy likes to fly airplanes, go fishing, keep books at his desk and ring in the New Year. Father Christmas is one busy fellow!"

That's how Carol, her sister-in-law, Ruth, and Ruth's daughter, Misho, depict St. Nick in the original, life-like characters they create to highlight the holidays.

"Besides showing Santa in his red-suited best on December 24, we portray his daily life," Ruth cheerily reveals. "For instance, you'll see our jovial gent checking a globe for the fastest around-the-world route or playing a pretty tune on a piano.

"He may even be taking medicine to calm his stomach before the big ride," she chuckles, "or catching a well-deserved nap afterward!"

Fashioning happy North Pole souls has been the Vance clan's year-round activity since 1994, when Carol first designed a bunch of Kris Kringles as Christmas gifts for kin.

"They were so enthused, Ruth convinced me that we should keep making Santas," Carol tells. "We turned the building next to my house—which years ago had been my family's specialty meat market—into our Claus workshop."

There, these creative ladies form soft-sculpture bodies—up to 6 feet tall—using wire and dowels. Heads and hands are shaped with clay and painted before faces are finished with fluffy lamb's-wool beards and old-fashioned eyeglasses.

Clothing of vintage and other material is sewn from original patterns. Finally, characters are accessorized with all sorts of trims—from antique goat wagons to bundles of birch twigs.

"Though our Nicks aren't toys, we call them 'action figures' because folks can pose them," smiles Misho. "They can sit on tables, hearths or shelves, and many can stand alone as the focal point in a room. We also make small elves that can cling to a tree, hang on a chair or sit in a wreath."

Since they began crafting their Santas, Carol, Ruth and Misho have seen the figures delight everyone from corporate executives to collectors and move from craft shows to gift shops and galleries—even a spot in the Museum of American Folk Art in New York City.

"That was quite a thrill for three girls with a glue gun," Carol laughs. "But one part has been the most satisfying of all—helping to make Christmas as special as can be."

Editor's Note: *For a brochure about the Vance family's Santas and elves, send a self-addressed stamped, business-size envelope to Images of Christmas, P.O. Box 116, Benton PA 17814, call 1-570/925-2591 or send a fax to 1/570-784-0555.*

THE CREATIVE Vance clan—Carol, Ruth and Misho (from left to right below)—has a merry time shaping soft-sculpture Santas and elves. Some even rise to 6 feet tall (above).

Retired Teacher's Homework Highlights Holiday Painting

NOWADAYS you won't find Carol Schmidt in school. But this ex-instructor still regularly brushes up on her favorite subject—Christmas!

"With my palette of paints, I decorate just about anything I can get hold of with bright designs celebrating Yuletide," smiles Carol from the creek-side cabin she shares with a fellow crafter her mother, Betty—in Goshen, Ohio.

"Garden produce, wood pieces, outdoor finds and more get a merry coat of color in the form of patchwork Santas, cheery cherubs, plump snow folks and jolly gingerbreads. In fact, nearly every bit of brushwork I do has a December theme."

Carol's love for Christmas is what led her to dabble in Noel motifs…but her schoolteacher's schedule for 36 years helped seal the deal.

"From fall to spring," she recalls, "I'd be busy with a class of kindergartners and didn't have many spare moments to do all the painting I wanted.

"But my summer vacations gave me lots of time. And since autumn bazaars were right around the corner, they got me focused on Yuletide," Carol notes. "You might say my 'Christmas break' came twice a year—once in December, then again from June to August!"

Setting the tone for Carol's illustrations are the objects she picks to trim, many of them straight from nature.

"Gourds of different shapes and sizes are high on my list—and involve the most preparation.

"After soaking them and scraping off the mold, I add two coats of gesso (a plaster-like compound), plus feet formed from putty if I'm making a whole body. Then I basecoat and apply a Claus or snowman with paint."

Carol embellishes pinecones by attaching elf faces she's molded with clay and mixes in accessories like Spanish moss, berries and ribbon. She also glosses over mini wooden sleds, tree ornaments, lapel pins and decorations for wreaths. "The more projects, the merrier," Carol chuckles.

"Custom orders I get from folks often add to my ideas. For example, once—for an optometrist—I needed a gourd depicting Kris Kringle wearing eyeglasses. Instead of *painting* the spectacles, I affixed real ones. Those Nicks are now my most popular."

And chances are, plenty of new pictorials featuring Noel are still to come.

"Since I've retired from teaching, I've become a full-time crafter," Carol affirms. "Christmas is always in my heart."

Editor's Note: *For more information, send a self-addressed stamped envelope to Carol Schmidt, 6231 Wald Lane, Goshen OH 45122, or call her at 1-513/625-6419.* 🔔

GOURDS, pinecones and other tidbits of nature inspire Carol Schmidt and her mother, Betty (above left), to paint up a seasonal storm.

Rich Wood

Her Midwest Barn Brings Christmas Past to Present

STRUCTURING holiday festivities around days gone by is a pastime Janis King happily shares with others out in her historic red barn.

"The weekend after Thanksgiving each year, we turn the barn into a craft gallery. Folks from all over flock to see the wares inside," Janis observes from the grain and livestock operation her family runs near Knoxville, Illinois.

When not decked out for the season, the Civil War-era barn houses hay, machinery and cattle. "This building has seen well over a century of Christmases," she sums up. "Nowadays, we like to take a trip back in time as we celebrate the season.

"As visitors arrive, Father Christmas welcomes them at the door. Once inside, they find stalls full of wares from local artisans, such as baskets, quilts, pottery, tinware, herb soaps, wood-carved Santas and jewelry."

Adding to the season's greetings she delights in supplying, Janis and her crafting pal, Ruby Bledsoe, design and sell wreaths, swags, roping and arrangements made from greenery, everlastings and other bits of nature.

"We also offer horse-drawn wagon and sleigh rides," Janis notes.

"After a refreshing country excursion, folks like to pick out their perfect Christmas trees from our lot of fresh-cut ones. Others come back to the barn to enjoy Christmas carols performed by local musicians."

Another seasonal treat is a groaning-with-goodies refreshment table featuring homemade soups and candies, herb breads and steaming cups of punch.

"We greet some 1,500 people from as far away as Kansas, California and Nebraska," Janis reveals. "Many have established Christmas at Walnut Grove Farm as an 'after-turkey' activity. Our barn's become a family tradition!"

Indeed, King family members are all wrapped up in the festivities, too. "My three sons, Seth, 22, and 17-year-old

twins Aaron and Nathan, help their Grandpa Leonard sell evergreens," Janis offers. "My sisters often travel from Oregon to help with the barn's decoration."

Making merry isn't a once-a-year proposition, however. The nostalgic barn is open to the public for summer weddings and reunions and autumn and winter craft shows, too.

"Hosting these fun events, particularly our Christmastime fair, is especially rewarding because of the old-fashioned setting," Janis concludes.

"With each new friend I meet, I have a chance to share the legacy of this barn and our farming heritage. That makes the holidays warmer for everyone."

Editor's Note: *Christmas at Walnut Grove Farm is held annually the weekend after Thanksgiving. The farm is located 1/2 mile north of Knoxville, Illinois on Carr Street. For more information, call Janis at 1-309/289-4770 or visit her Web site: www.walnutgrove farm.com.*

FATHER CHRISTMAS (at top) welcomes young and old to Janis King's idyllic Illinois barnyard. During Yule season, the historic red barn brims with holiday wares by area artisans. Janis (above left) and pal Ruby Bledsoe turn to nature for all their crafty creations.

Sculptor Coins St. Nicks That Enrich the Season

Enesco Group Inc.

WHEN IT COMES to spreading holiday cheer, the Kris Kringles shaped by Linda Lindquist Baldwin are right on the money…in more ways than one!

To begin with, the decorative "Belsnickle" characters she creates with papier-mache bring back the Old World beauty of past Santas. And embedded in the base of each figure, you'll find a real nickel.

"The coin commemorates how I started sculpting," shares this merry Joplin, Missouri wife and mother. "Until 15 years ago, I hadn't even thought about molding these Nicks."

That is, until Linda was shopping at a garage sale and came across a 5¢ book. "It dealt with antique papier-mache Santas worth thousands of dollars.

"Paging through it, I loved the look of each Claus but knew I couldn't afford one," Linda recalls.

"So I made up my mind to craft some

myself, learning as I went along."

Based on the centuries-old German Santa called Belsnickel (Linda changed the spelling of hers), Linda's richly textured figures depict an old-fashioned kind of Claus who could be both kind and strict.

"According to legend, he brought sweets or toys to nice children—and sticks or lumps of coal to naughty ones," she describes.

The wealth of artwork she does also includes English Father Christmases, American Santas and nautical Nicks, as well as snowmen and Halloween characters she cleverly calls "Snowsnickles" and "Broomsnickles". Pieces range from figurines and ornaments to bells and wall masks.

"I make dozens of projects—up to 12 inches tall—each year," Linda tallies. "Preparing the papier-mache is my first step. I soak newspaper for several weeks, then beat it with a mallet into an oatmeal-like consistency.

"Once I start sculpting, I don't stop to eat or sleep, even for as long as 30 hours," she adds with a grin. "I like to keep my creative juices flowing without interruption!"

When drying is complete—which takes up to 2 months—Linda applies acrylic paint and trims like pinecones, berries or creek stones she's gathered at the Ozark farm where she grew up, 50 miles from her current home.

With her sizable "coin" collection, it's no surprise Linda's good fortune shows up throughout her household. "I keep my Santas out all year in every room," she admits. "My husband, Bill, and grown son, Seth, have never seemed to mind.

"In fact, years ago, Seth summed up my crafting perfectly: 'From a nickel to the Belsnickle'," Linda smiles. "It's truly been a wonderful way to 'spend' Christmas."

Editor's Note: *To find a shop near you that carries Linda's Belsnickles, Snowsnickles or Broomsnickles, call Enesco at 1-800-NEAR-YOU.* 🔔

SEASON'S TREASURES. Linda Lindquist Baldwin (above left) found good fortune in papier-mache. Her Santas are rich with detail.

Christmastime Was Full of Treasured Family Traditions

By Marian Miley of Ravenna, Ohio

IT'S LIKELY no surprise that the most anticipated holiday back when I was a child was Christmas. Times were simpler, though, and our celebrations were mostly focused on family.

In fact, much of what we did on December 25 revolved around long-standing traditions involving kinfolk. One such custom I particularly looked forward to was our annual trek to our grandparents', whom we affectionately called Baba and Gido, for Christmas dinner.

Depending on whose car was in good working order, ours or Uncle Ben's, we'd fill it with boxes of food, bags stuffed with gifts and plenty of excited youngsters!

Driving regulations and seat belts didn't exist—we'd all just pile in on top of each other. Anyone lucky enough to get an actual spot to sit held a smaller person or package on his or her lap.

Although most of the meats, potatoes, desserts and kolachi were packed into the trunk, delicious aromas soon wafted into the auto. We didn't have tin foil or Tupperware back then—we made do with newspaper and covered dishes.

Mingling with those mouth-watering scents were the unmistakable odors of wet wool and galoshes. Of course, we didn't notice smells of any kind when the heater wasn't working…nor did we feel the cold. Excitement kept us cozy!

Laughing All the Way

The adults would talk about world affairs, new recipes and new babies, while the children buzzed about presents and school. We all sang songs and chuckled at the glove that took the place of the radiator cap.

Sometimes the car would vibrate, and our young voices would do the same, much to our delight. Then one of the mothers would say, "Hush!"—and we'd try to stifle our giggles.

Our trip wouldn't be complete without the vehicle stalling at least once or twice. Somehow, the menfolk always managed to get the touchy automobile started again.

As we approached Baba and Gido's house on the hill, we'd urge the car up the incline with our prayers until, with a slip, slide, jerk and roll, we'd reach the top once more.

Then we'd all help unload the goodies before

walking carefully up the steps and into the small warm house, where we were greeted with even more flavorful fragrances—chicken soup, roast turkey and pies galore.

After hugs and kisses, we were treated to such greetings as "My goodness, you've grown a foot" or "What a cute little tyke". Then it was time to eat!

No one cared that dishes and silverware didn't match or that we sat on a blend of chairs from the kitchen and the dining room (even the rocking chair got put to use!). We were just grateful for what we had and for each other, and we thanked God for all our blessings.

Since the dining room wasn't big enough to accommodate all of us, the adults ate first. When the dishes were cleared, we kids crammed around the table and filled our plates.

I can still see the beautiful ruby goblets Baba always put out. As much as I disliked milk, I gladly drank glassfuls from one of those cups!

Sharing the Wealth

After everyone had eaten their fill and all the dishes were washed, it was time for our most "rewarding" tradition.

Each year, Uncle Paul kept change in an old cigar box until Christmas, when he'd pass it out to the children. We'd all thank him and excitedly describe how we'd spend our fortune on new games, roller skates, dolls and the like.

In my immediate family, it was our habit to compile the coins and let Mom and Dad use them for something we all could enjoy. I'm not sure what our cousins did with their cash, but I have a feeling it was handled in the same way.

Once we settled down, everyone gathered around to talk and relax. Sometimes, Aunt Dorothy would suddenly recall a gift she'd "forgotten", usually a Parcheesi game for the boys or a bunch of little dolls for the girls.

Finally, after the last piece of pie was finished, we'd bundle up and pile into the car, filling the interior with the smells of leftovers, new mittens and the pungent peppermint candies Gido gave us.

The adults talked more quietly during this ride, and the old jalopy rattled along, rocking most of us to sleep.

I wouldn't be surprised if we all dreamed the same dreams—of good food, ruby glasses, the old cigar box bursting with coins and plenty of love to go around for everyone!

Farm Clan's Bright Display Shines a Light on Holidays

COME CHRISTMAS, Doris Nanninga's all aglow—and so are the fields she farms with husband Lee near Morrowville, Kansas!

This jolly lady, along with Lee and grown son Rusty, sparks the spirit of the season by fashioning a brilliant display of lights that covers 6 acres…and attracts folks from all over.

"People travel as much as 100 miles to see our Christmas Joyland. On a busy night, we can get as many as 150 carloads rolling up our drive," Doris says.

"What makes the display so special is the fact that we've made many of the items ourselves. It gives me a great sense of accomplishment every time we flip the switch."

This Yuletide highlight got its start some 20 years ago when Rusty was in grade school. "He strung a single strand of lights around the living room window and added two plastic Noel candles to our doorstep," recalls his mother.

"We charged ahead the following year and wrapped our home, barn, outbuildings, fences and trees with twinkling lights," Doris continues.

From there, the clan grounded their efforts by attaching bulbs to netting similar to chicken wire to form a miniature holiday village patterned after buildings in Morrowville.

"Using that same technique, we made a miniature toy train complete with a depot and a life-size Santa and sleigh with reindeer," Doris describes. "We've also included wooden figures, animated items, a Nativity and lots more!"

One favorite is the Christmas carousel adorning a granary. "We created cutouts of elves on reindeer and attached motion lights so everything looks like it's moving," she details.

"The carousel holds 1,000 lights. We use 35,000 to 40,000 lights total, fueled by 2 miles of underground wiring.

"It takes us about a month to set up everything," notes Doris. "And each year, we add new scenes. Our daughter, Lori, and her husband lend a hand with the construction.

"Then Lori and Rusty make cookies and pass out the treats to visitors. Even our grandson, Chandler, helps out any way he can. It's a fun family affair.

"Christmas Joyland is really all about giving," smiles Doris. "It's about the groups of seniors who delight in the sights, the excited children and the letters we receive expressing sincere appreciation for our efforts.

"Most of all, it's about spreading Christmas cheer and remembering what the season is all about."

Editor's Note: *No fee is charged to see Christmas Joyland, although free-will donations are accepted.*

The display is open November 23-24 (call ahead for times), December 1 and December 8-31. Hours during December are 6-10 p.m. on Sundays and weekdays and 6-10:30 p.m. Saturdays and December 24-25 and 31.

The farm is located 12 miles west of Washington on U.S. 36 or 25 miles east of Belleville. For details, contact Doris Nanninga, 913 15th Rd., Morrowville KS 66958; 1-785/265-3538.

SPARKING a scene each Christmas is Doris Nanninga's happy habit. Doris (top left) and family string up farm with loads of lights and festive sights for visitors from all over to enjoy.

Country Crafter Finds Her Yule Spirit 'Claus' to Home

BARBARA SHOOP has a real talent for stopping Santa in his tracks. In fact, this creative lady captures him quite handily.

"For me, Father Christmas is not just a visitor who turns up in December," says the seasoned Santa maker from Dayton, Wyoming. "He's a year-round holiday presence."

Several Santa sightings have been reported in Barbara's guest bedroom-turned-whimsical workshop.

A velvet-vested Father Christmas fills his pack on one table, while a Nick in denim saddles up atop another. An aproned Mrs. Claus collects holly in the corner, and a festive frontiersman looks out the window at the mountains.

"Our country surroundings inspire many of my one-of-a-kind figures," Barbara notes, nodding at a jolly ol' cowboy, skier, woodsman and bird-watcher. "My dolls range from 13 to 19 inches high, and each has a lifelike twinkle in his eye."

Barbara began her character-building efforts 12 years ago, when she started fashioning the detailed Noel fellows for friends. Since then, local gift shops and customers from across the country have added her clever Clauses to their wish lists.

"I start by mounting a Styrofoam cone on a stained wood base," she cheerfully explains.

"Next I attach posable wire arms and commercial porcelain head and hands, before creating a well-rounded personality with cotton batting.

"His trademark whiskers are formed from natural sheep's wool I comb into flowing curls. And seeing as Santa's a world traveler, I might stitch him an ethnic costume or custom-sew a cloak from a cherished heirloom quilt a customer provides me."

Routinely, Barbara frequents flea markets, rummage sales and second-hand stores seeking accents for the bearded man of her dreams.

Much like the elf himself, she's always on the lookout for accessories to dress up her characters—tiny toys, trees, baskets, beads, sleigh bells and sleds included.

"Often, my husband, Alva, and I gather pinecones for trimmings in our Big Horn Mountains," she enthuses. "Mother Nature and Father Christmas make a beautiful couple."

It's obvious, Barbara's Yule heirlooms have a true family feeling behind them. "Our three young grandchildren love to watch me make what they call 'Grandma's Ho-Ho's'" she chuckles. "They consider Santa a real member of our household."

So if you have any doubts about the very merriest of characters, Barbara is only too glad to make a believer out of you, too!

Editor's Note: *If you'd like information on her original Father Christmas creations, send a self-addressed stamped envelope to Barbara Shoop, P.O. Box 354, Dayton WY 82836 or phone 1-307/655-9381.*

FLEA MARKET FINDS accent the Father Christmas figures created by Barbara Shoop (at top). She also scouts rummage sales and second-hand stores for trees, toys, beads and bells to dress up her one-of-a-kind world travelers for that all-important sleigh ride through the sky.

TASTY-LOOKING TRIMS turn Linda Himes' cozy country home into a sweet holiday feast Hansel and Gretel would love. Linda (below) even constructs a matching cookie cottage.

Sugar and Spice Help Make Her Country House Extra Nice

LIFE IS SWEET at Linda Himes' rural address in Kersey, Pennsylvania...particularly at Christmas!

"Most of the year, our simple country house is just that—a cozy but modest home," describes Linda from her woodsy neighborhood. "There's no lavish landscaping or sprawling square footage to make for a showy place.

"But as soon as the holiday season nears, I cook up my own home-baked cheer," she says. "I transform our brown-and-white exterior into a gingerbread house, just like the kind folks concoct in the kitchen."

Those edible abodes are what whetted Linda's appetite for decorating. "In a 1998 issue of *Country Woman* magazine, I saw some truly beautiful cookie creations," she reveals. "I thought dreamily, 'How wonderful it would be to actually live in one!'

"And that inspired me to craft outdoor trims resembling *CW's* sugary confections."

In Linda's tasteful display, striped treats line the woodwork above a porch with peppermint posts...friendly gingerbreads spice up the entranceway and underneath the windows...and a pair

of chocolate kisses tempt around the front steps.

Flavoring the arrangement even more are wrapped hard candies bordering the door, red and green canes near the corners and icing icicles that droop from the roof.

"The whole project cost only $25 to do," Linda happily tallies, "since my 'ingredients' included plenty of on-hand scraps.

"For example, I covered cardboard cutouts with aluminum foil to form the kisses and embellished Styrofoam with ribbon to produce peppermint sticks. Old paint and colorful cellophane came in handy, too."

For much of the frosting, Linda relies on another accomplished "cook". "Mother Nature layers snow on the bushes and rooftop," she winks. "My decor isn't complete without that finishing touch. Luckily—in our northern area—I can always count on it!"

Linda's husband, John, a machine designer and builder, helps her reassemble the goodies each year. "Our children, John, Clint, Alicia and Ashley, tell everyone that they live in 'the gingerbread house'—and share pictures

with all who haven't seen it," Linda chuckles.

It didn't take long for word of mouth to spread, either, Linda notes. "Come Christmas, cars drive by for a 'sample' of our scene at all hours, since we have lights that illuminate the yard at night."

In honor of her luscious lodging, Linda whips up a matching cookie abode that resembles her real one. "I plan to keep preparing my life-size 'recipe', too," she smiles. "After all, it's a warm, sweet feeling to live in a gingerbread house."

Editor's Note: *If you'd like to view Lina Himes' Christmas-trimmed home, feel free to drive by! Her address is 118 Lovers Lane in Kersey, Pennslyvania. Decorations stay up throughout the season.*

Christmas Wreath

First, twist on some holly,
Then sprays of pretty pine,
A balsam branch, some cedar,
And partridgeberry vine;

Tuck in glossy acorns,
A spray of mistletoe,
Then cones of pine and hemlock,
And last—a big red bow!

—Edith E. Cutting
Johnson City, New York

May the delightful sights and sounds of Christmas fill you and yours with joy the whole year through.

INDEX

 ## Share Your Holiday Joy!

DO *YOU* celebrate Christmas in a special way? If so, we'd like to know! We're already gathering material for our next *Country Woman Christmas* book. And we need your help!

Do you have a nostalgic holiday-related story to share? Perhaps you have penned a Christmas poem…or a heart-warming fiction story?

Does your family carry on a favorite holiday tradition? Or do you deck your halls in some festive way? Maybe you know of a Christmas-loving country woman others might like to meet?

We're looking for *original* Christmas quilt patterns and craft projects, too, plus homemade Nativities, gingerbread houses, etc. Don't forget to include your best recipes for holiday-favorite main-dish meats, home-baked cookies, candies, breads, etc.!

Send your ideas and photos to "*CW* Christmas Book", 5925 Country Lane, Greendale WI 53129. (Enclose a self-addressed stamped envelope if you'd like materials returned.)